Into the Unknown

Praise for this book

'This is a wonderful book of deep insight, sharp reflection and above all a renewed call to action. Robert Chambers is one of the great explorers of our age, brave enough to pass into new landscapes of thought and ideas, capable enough to explain how poor people could live their lives if only they had the opportunity.'

Jules Pretty, Professor of Environment and Society, University of Essex

'This is a fascinating and inspiring journey into participation, learning and social transformation. Chambers is a quintessential practitioner, thinker, learner and provocateur. I believe that this latest addition to Robert's collection will stimulate a new generation of development practitioners in an era of "doom and gloom" today.'

Dr Rajesh Tandon, founder and President of Participatory Research in Asia

'Robert Chambers introduces us to an art of exploratory rock climbing called "development practice" – a practice that knows many teachers. Few, however, show the humour and self-reflexivity of Chambers in these profoundly humanist memoirs by a unique development practitioner.'

Louk Box, former Rector of the International Institute of Social Studies, and a Distinguished Fellow at the University of South Africa's Chair in Development Education

'With his infectious optimism and lucid, insightful – and often highly entertaining – prose, Robert Chambers has given us yet another book that is set to become a classic. Of all his works, this is my favourite, not only for its reflexive engagement and for the inspiring example Robert gives us of looking for lessons from where things went wrong, but also for what it exhorts us to do: to engage our imaginations, our passions and our curiosity to create a better, fairer world.'

Andrea Cornwall, Professor of Anthropology and International Development, University of Sussex, UK

'A brilliant book. Robert Chambers draws on his personal journeys in rural development to provide searing insights into the pervasive blind spots and myths that hamper development efforts worldwide, and ways to overcome them. *Into the Unknown* will inspire both seasoned and burgeoning explorers in rural development and encourage them to find truer pathways forward.'

Roberto Lenton, founding Executive Director, Robert B. Daugherty Water for Food Institute, University of Nebraska

'In this book, Robert Chambers refers to himself as "an explorer" and poignantly reflects on his incredible half-century career of "exploration". Like other great explorers, Robert has opened new frontiers – of knowledge, methodology, self-reflection and learning. In this latest book, he inspires and challenges other development practitioners also to become explorers – not to follow his path, but to create their own paths towards a new 21st-century development project.'

John Gaventa, Director, Coady International Institute, St Francis Xavier University, Canada, and Professor, Institute of Development Studies, University of Sussex

Into the Unknown
Explorations in
development practice

Robert Chambers

PRACTICAL ACTION
Publishing

Practical Action Publishing Ltd
The Schumacher Centre
Bourton on Dunsmore, Rugby,
Warwickshire CV23 9QZ, UK
www.practicalactionpublishing.org

ISBN 978-1-85339-822-3 Hardback
ISBN 978-1-85339-823-0 Paperback
ISBN 978-1-78044-822-0 Library Ebook
ISBN 978-1-78044-823-7 Ebook

Chambers, R. (2014) *Into the Unknown: Explorations in
Development Practice*, Rugby, UK: Practical Action Publishing
<http://dx.doi.org/10.3362/9781780448220>.

Since 1974, Practical Action Publishing has published and disseminated
books and information in support of international development work
throughout the world. Practical Action Publishing is a trading name of
Practical Action Publishing Ltd (Company Reg. No. 1159018), the wholly
owned publishing company of Practical Action. Practical Action Publishing
trades only in support of its parent charity objectives and any profits
are covenanted back to Practical Action (Charity Reg. No. 247257,
Group VAT Registration No. 880 9924 76).

Cover design by Mercer Design
Indexed by Liz Fawcett, Harrogate, UK
Typeset by Marie Doherty
Printed in the United Kingdom

FSC

MIX

Paper

FSC® C014540

Contents

About the author

Professor Robert Chambers is a research associate of the Institute of Development Studies, at the University of Sussex, UK, which has been his base since 1969 with periods in other countries. His educational background is in natural sciences, history and public administration. His main administrative and research experience in development has been in East Africa and South Asia. Among other work he has been a field administrator and trainer of administrators in Kenya and East Africa, a field researcher in Kenya, India and Sri Lanka, an evaluation officer with UNHCR and a project specialist with the Ford Foundation in India.

Books he has written include *Rural Development: Putting the Last First* (1983), *Challenging the Professions* (1993), *Whose Reality Counts? Putting the First Last* (1997), *Participatory Workshops* (2002), *Ideas for Development* (2005), *Revolutions in Development Inquiry* (2008) and *Provocations for Development* (2012). His current work and interests include participatory methodologies; participation, power and complexity; professional perceptions and the realities of poverty and well-being; and going to scale with community-led total sanitation.

Abbreviations and acronyms

CGIAR	Consultative Group for International Agricultural Research
CIAT	International Centre for Tropical Agriculture
CLTS	community-led total sanitation
COP	community of practice
DFID	Department for International Development (UK)
ICRISAT	International Crops Research Institute for the Semi-arid Tropics
IDS	Institute of Development Studies at the University of Sussex, UK
IIED	International Institute for Environment and Development
IIMI	International Irrigation Management Institute
INGO	international non-governmental organization
IPM	integrated pest management
KIA	Kenya Institute of Administration
LSE	London School of Economics
LSHTM	London School of Hygiene and Tropical Medicine
NGO	non-governmental organization
ODA	Overseas Development Administration (UK)
ODF	open defecation free
PPA	participatory poverty assessment
PRA	participatory rural appraisal
PW	*Participatory Workshops* book (Chambers, 2002)
RRA	rapid rural appraisal
SIDA now Sida	Swedish International Development Cooperation Agency
SDC	Swiss Agency for Development and Cooperation
SOSOTEC	self-organizing systems on the edge of chaos
SRDP	Special Rural Development Programme
UNHCR	United Nations High Commissioner for Refugees
WSP	Water and Sanitation Program of the World Bank

Preface

One of the slogans or injunctions of PRA (participatory rural appraisal, sometimes participatory reflection and action) is 'Hand over the stick'. Again and again I have found that when I hand over the stick to others they do better than I would have done, and there are surprises and new things to learn. Repeatedly, in the feedback at the end of day-long workshops (Chapter 4) with 'students', who are really co-learners, sharers and co-generators of knowledge, the responses to 'what was best, what was most useful?' name not my sessions but those which participants facilitated, sharing their experiences.

Once at IDS (the Institute of Development Studies at the University of Sussex where I have been based for some time) a student participant, Steadman Noble, volunteered an exercise about our personal identities. He had each of us draw a diagram (Figure 0.1). We were to fill in the outer circles with who we were – man, father, rock climber (nostalgically), whatever – and then reflect on a core identity and write that in the middle. This was new to me. You might want to do it for yourself. I was startled – it was one of those ahha! moments of discovery which are a recurring theme in this book – to find myself writing in the word 'explorer'.

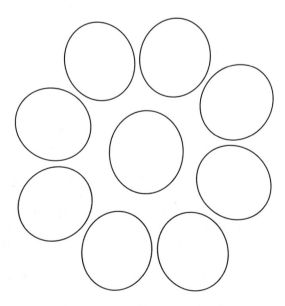

Figure 0.1 Personal identities (create more circles if required)

So was that at the centre of who I was? Or was that just how I liked to think of myself and present myself? Had my life really been, and did it continue to be, a life of exploring, venturing into unknown territory? Writing that now, it sounds pretentious. But then to a degree all of us are explorers, all of us are constantly entering the unknown. Living is continuous exploration. It is part of the human condition, intensified by consciousness and self-reflection. I liked having 'explorer' as a core identity, though ashamed that it was not more family and relationship-oriented. To me it was a flattering self-image; never mind the flip side: that most of those who are normally described as explorers are also escapers, running away from something. I could tell myself that it was the quality of what they experienced that counted. That I was running away from settling down after graduation from university did not diminish my experience of going with friends on an expedition to Gough Island in the South Atlantic, hoping to explore physically in the classical sense.[1] And I could remember that many of the most intense and exhilarating times of my life had been exploratory climbing on rock where others had not been before.[2] Writing, too, is an exploration: I realize and discover things through writing that I would never realize or discover otherwise.

So I tell myself that this book has itself been written in a spirit of exploration. Part I, 'Exploring experience', is about personal experiences: of a physical and disciplinary nomad in development studies (Chapter 1); of collaboration in a large-scale research project on poverty in 23 countries (Chapter 2); and of a wandering participant observer of the management of water and irrigation in South Asia (Chapter 3). The title 'Exploring experience' can and should be read two ways: as explorations of experiences, examining and trying to gain useful insights from them; and as critical reflections on the experience of exploring.

Part II, 'Exploring learning', is about a learning journey: learning about learning (Chapter 4), learning about participatory workshops for teaching and learning (Chapter 5), and for sharing and cogenerating knowledges (Chapter 6). Each of these chapters has an appendix of 21 methods, lessons or tips that have emerged and which I hope some readers will try out and find useful. These are à la carte menus of options for practices. The title 'Exploring learning' can and should be read two ways: as exploration of processes of learning, and as learning about exploring.

Part III, 'Into the new unknown', draws the book together with a forward look in Chapter 7 to exploring for our faster future world.

I have planned *Into the Unknown* as a companion and complement to another book tentatively entitled *Knowing in Development: Errors, Omissions and Insights*, which will draw on other sources and cover a different range of topics.

In a sense *Into the Unknown* has many authors: it draws on experiences and learning to which many, many colleagues, friends and family have contributed. It is, though, to a degree autobiographical and vulnerable to personal biases, not least fond delusions that practices have been effective when critical feedback might have shown otherwise. I ask myself why I have written it. We are adept at rationalizing and presenting the self in a gratifying light. So I tell myself that I would like to encourage, incite and provoke others to enjoy the thrills of exploring new territory, new experiences, new practices, new ways of doing things, new emotions, by seeking out, augmenting and exploiting more and more room for manoeuvre, more and more space for freedom and choice. I tell myself that, though readers will not be as lucky as me, I would like them to feel that they can seize fate by the throat, push at confining boundaries, and make themselves a bit luckier; and that they will know and feel for themselves some of the excitement and fulfilment that I have had. I tell myself that for all of us every experience is unique and new. It is here and now, today: every moment, every hour, every day can be an exploration if we choose to see it as such.

So the book ends, 'We can all be explorers'. But who are the 'we'? In a broad sense, all motile creatures are explorers, moving around and investigating their environments. Human consciousness adds a dimension of awareness and reflection on oneself. Among humankind there are huge disparities in freedom, resources and capacity to explore and experience. For many, this is constrained by poverty, physical weakness, vulnerability, confining norms and social relations and other dimensions of powerlessness. The 'we' addressed in this book are a minority, privileged people who are less constrained. A bottom line question for us is whether our development practices can lead to a fairer and better world for those with fewer freedoms and less choice.

For those of us who work in development, this is deadly serious. There are many terrible human tragedies. But that should not be all. A takeaway message from this book is that exploring development practices can be not just serious but stimulating, fulfilling and fun. I hope readers will join me in finding this.

Notes

1. See Holdgate, 1958.
2. By humans, as far as known. Some of the rocks in Kenya have been so extensively climbed by many generations of baboons that they have acquired a slippery polish that makes them treacherous for less prehensile primates.

Acknowledgements

Grateful acknowledgement is given to the original publishers to reproduce earlier writing as follows:

Zed Books for Chapter 1, which originally appeared as 'Critical reflections of a development nomad' in Kothari (2005: 67–87). I remain grateful to Uma Kothari for having invited and encouraged me to write this, and for her constructive critical comments on drafts.

Earthscan for Chapter 2, which originally appeared as 'Power, knowledge and policy influence: Reflections on an experience' in Karen Brock and Rosemary McGee (2002: 135–65). For stimulating comments presenting a range of views, suggestions and corrections based on drafts I remain grateful to Karen Brock, John Gaventa, Rosemary McGee, Deepa Narayan, Andrew Norton, Raj Patel, Patti Petesch, Jules Pretty, and Meera Kaul Shah. The experience with 'Consultations with the Poor', and the time to write this, were supported by DFID, SDC and Sida.

Water Alternatives for Chapter 3 which was published as 'Viewpoint – ignorance, error and myth in South Asian irrigation: Critical reflections on experience' (Chambers, 2013: 154–67). I thank Gilbert Levine and the other editors, Mercy Dikito-Wachtmeister and Miguel Solanes, for inviting me to write this, and Roberto Lenton and Gilbert Levine for constructive comments and information.

The Institute of Development Studies for parts of Chapter 6, which has been abbreviated, rewritten and added to for this book, from 'Sharing and co-generating knowledges: reflections on experiences with PRA and CLTS' in Burns (2012). I am grateful to Danny Burns for having encouraged me to write the original article, and for constructive comments on drafts to Alfredo Ortiz Aragon, Petra Bongartz, Danny Burns, Naomi Hossain, Rosie McGee, Jethro Pettit, Patta Scott-Villiers and Stephen Wood.

Chapters 4, 5 and 7 are new for this book.

My thanks go to Sulu Mathew and Jenny Jackman for their prompt and accurate work on the text and support in other ways: they made the later stages of writing much less arduous and much more enjoyable than they might have been. For copy-editing I am grateful to Jane Boughton and for the index to Liz Fawcett. Thanks go to the Participation, Power and Social Change team in IDS for supporting this publication. Toby Milner and Clare Tawney of Practical Action Publishing have given much appreciated encouragement, and comments and suggestions throughout, and these have led to more revisions than they may have expected. Rewriting has been more thorough and has taken longer than I ever imagined it would. Above all, throughout the years Jenny Chambers has been a wonderful companion and contributor of ideas in so many ways. Without her, this and other books could never have been written.

Robert Chambers

PART I

Exploring experience

CHAPTER 1

Critical reflections of a development nomad

This is a critical account of personal nomadism wandering on the boundaries of disciplines and exploring gaps between them. It sets the scene for the rest of the book by showing where I come from, what I am not, and where I have been, including episodes as a colonial administrator, trainer and researcher in Kenya, lecturer who never lectured, evaluation programme manager (failed), field researcher in South Asia, evaluation officer in Geneva, project specialist for the Ford Foundation, and later, collaborator, networker and disseminator of participatory methodologies, most of the time with a base at the Institute of Development Studies, University of Sussex.

Keywords: critical reflection, development studies, development studies research, freedom, funding constraints, methodologies, opportunism, optimizing reflexivity and managing ego, participation, participatory workshops, pedagogy for the powerful, personal mindset, power and error, radical agenda, reversals, self-critical epistemological awareness

> **Nomad** *n* **1** a member of a people or tribe who move from place to place to find pasture and food **2** a person who continually moves from place to place; wanderer.
>
> *Collins English Dictionary Millennium Edition*

Prologue

The Egocentric Reminiscence Ratio (ERR) (the proportion of a person's speech devoted to their past – 'when I was ...' and 'I remember when ...' etc.) is supposedly higher among men than women, rises with age, on retirement leaps to a new high level, is higher in the evening than the morning, and rises sharply with the consumption of alcohol. Since in what follows my ERR is close to 100 per cent, let me assure any reader that I am sober and that I rarely work after seven in the evening. I am writing this less because of the compulsions of age, gender and ego (though of course they are there) and more (or so I would like to flatter myself by believing) because I have been asked to. All the same, writing about your experience is an indulgence. The only justification is if it makes a difference – whether through others' pleasure, insight or action, or through your own personal change.

Most of my working life I have been based at the Institute of Development Studies, Sussex, but much of this has been abroad. I have experienced and

http://dx.doi.org/10.3362/9781780448220.001

lived through changes in development studies, but not in any mainstream. As an undisciplined non-economist, I have been on the fringes. In consequence, my view of development studies is idiosyncratic. Writing this has helped me to understand myself a little better. Others will judge whether it is of interest or use to them.

What have reflections on personal experience to do with development studies, and what might be radical about this? Answers to these questions vary according to how broad development studies is taken to be, and what is taken to be radical.

The scope of development studies can be broad in two respects. First, empirically, it can refer to what people in centres, departments or institutes of, or for, development studies actually do and have done. In the UK, development studies has also to embrace whatever the Development Studies Association considers, names or explores. What people do or have done includes not just research and teaching, but consultancy, advisory work, dissemination, advocacy, convening, networking and partnerships. Some in development studies have also spent time as volunteers, or in governments, aid agencies, NGOs and foundations.

Second, normatively, if development is defined as good change, development studies are again broad. Values have always been there in the discourses of development even if often half hidden by pretences of objectivity. Introducing values expands the boundaries beyond, for example, what one may find in a book on development economics or social development, and includes ethics, individual choice and responsibility. What is *good* is then for individual and collective definition and debate, as is what sorts of change are significant.

The reader can judge whether it is radical or not to take these two broad meanings together and reflect critically on what someone in development studies does in a lifetime.[1] To help and warn, the least I can do in my case is describe the more significant predispositions (aka biases, prejudices and blind spots) of which I am aware.[2] I am an optimistic nomad. My spectacles are rose-coloured. Pessimists may be justified in claiming more realism. For whatever reasons, cups to me are more often half full than half empty.[3] Life is more enjoyable this way, and I have a fond and possibly delusional belief that naïve optimism has a wonderful way of being self-fulfilling. Enthusiasm is another weakness, bringing with it the dangers of selective perception, and of doing harm when combined with power.

As for being a nomad, it would be flattering to explain this in terms of a drive to *explore*; and when writing I like to use that word. But I have been running away more than running to. I have run away from whatever was dull, difficult or conflictual. This has meant avoiding the challenges in the heartland of any discipline or profession and instead seeking life and livelihood in other, emptier spaces. Being nomadic and marginal like this has been exhilarating, fulfilling and fun, a mix of solitary wandering and collegial solidarity with others in a small tribe. But when the tribe grows, it is time to move on.

Two themes – reflexivity and choosing what to do – are threaded through this account. They are hidden in Section 2, 'Nomad and journey', which the reader may wish to skip, come into the open in Section 3, 'Reflections', and finally inform Section 4, 'A radical agenda for development studies'. This last draws on the preceding critical reflection to ask what are some of the things we – development professionals with one or more feet in development studies – should try to do in the future.

Nomad and journey

The five phases which follow are separated for purposes of description but were experienced as a flow.

Uprooting and running away

I was born and brought up in a small English provincial town (Cirencester). My parents were middle class, both thwarted in their education. My mother had fought for more years in school, but still got less than her brothers. My father's schooling was downgraded and shortened when his father lost his cattle and farm to foot-and-mouth. I think they passed their frustrations on to me. I do not regret it. I was sent to prep school and to boarding public school. These were followed by National Service and university. My script was to come top in school, to be a good little boy basking in approval, and go on and on to become Prime Minister or Director-General of the BBC. In the jargon of an earlier social science, I had a high N-Ach or need for achievement.

From early on, though, I wandered, pulling up roots and moving on. After School Certificate (GCSEs) I did a year of mathematics, then switched to botany, chemistry and zoology for A-levels, then to history at university, and then to public administration, becoming, as I have happily remained, undisciplined. Ever since university I have been running, and running away, never staying for long in one place or with one subject. I ran away from a safe family firm of estate agents in provincial England. I went on a scientific expedition with friends to Gough Island in the South Atlantic (Holdgate, 1958). Then there was a year in the USA on an English-Speaking Union scholarship studying for an aborted PhD on changes in the American ideal of success. I ran on then to my first regular job, in Kenya as a District Officer in what was known by then (1958) as Her Majesty's Overseas Civil Service. I made it clear that I was only interested if I could be spared another year at Cambridge on what was known as a Devonshire Course. This was sort of proto-development studies for those going into colonial administration; it included history, social anthropology and other subjects considered relevant. And that was how I got into 'development'.

Decolonizing

It is difficult to convey to others the exhilaration of the decolonizing experience in Kenya (Johnson, 2002). As a District Officer I would have been seen by some as a wicked colonialist. I am not here defending or glossing any of the outrages of colonialism. But the task then was to prepare for independence and one could not have wished for a better job.

Whether for my supposed left-wing political views, or because of my love of mountains,[4] I shall never know, but I was posted for two and a half years to the remote Samburu District in Northern Kenya, where I was told there was 'no politics'. There was work as a third-class magistrate, administering tribal police, and a great deal of walking and riding horses. The most constructive part was finding dam sites, building dams and managing grazing control to save the Samburu pastoralists from destroying their environment. Or so I believed. This was followed by North Tetu Division in Nyeri District, where people were exploding with energy, and work included negotiating sites for new primary schools when existing ones exceeded their size limit, encouraging coffee planting, and getting tree seedlings to people who insatiably seized them to plant on their consolidated land.

There were then two big challenges in Kenya: training for the takeover of government with independence; and settlement of Africans on the former White Highlands. I wanted to get involved in one or the other. Because I was a mountaineer, and had accompanied a training course on Mount Kenya, the door opened to be a trainer. I was recruited to the new Kenya Institute of Administration (KIA) and was responsible for three back-to-back six-month courses for Kenyan administrators who were taking over. This was an extraordinarily intense experience, innovating and improvising on the run, and beginning to learn how to avoid having to lecture: this was anyway essential as I did know enough about anything to be able to talk about it for any length of time. The last course of 24 graduates straight from university, mainly Makerere in Uganda, challenged ('Why do we need to climb Kilimanjaro in order to be able to run our country?') but did not subvert the somewhat muscular approach of the training, which stressed character and self-confidence. The subjects covered included law, accounting, government procedures, natural resources, making district plans in real districts, and aspects of public administration covering all major ministries and departments (see Fuller, 2002: 240–3). We put together practical case studies using real government files with the names unchanged. Through these, trainees dealt with real problems and could compare their solutions and the memos they wrote with those of known senior colonial officers (Chambers, 1964). Another exercise was dealing with an overloaded in tray which we trainers had much fun composing. One of my subjects was politics, for which I concentrated on European pathologies as sources of lessons.[5] For better or for worse this was probably the most influential six months of my life (several on the courses were Permanent Secretaries in under two years). Then suddenly there was no one left to train. De-Europeanization had been so fast that Kenyans could no longer be spared for training. Kenya was independent and I was put in charge of the KIA library. It was time to move on.

Retreading and research

After rejecting the idea of a career in politics in the UK (the Liberal Party, which I supported, was in deep, possibly terminal, decline), I opted, as did a few others, to retrain as an academic, registered for a part-time PhD at Manchester under W.J.M. (Bill) Mackenzie, and joined Guy Hunter, who was launching the East African Staff College.[6] We ran three-week courses in Nairobi, Kampala and Dar-es-Salaam in rotation, for senior civil servants and business managers. We began asking participants to make population projections to 1980, and debated disbelief at the dramatic rises in rural as well as urban populations. Government and business case studies played a part, as did talks and discussions with political leaders. My 'research' narrowed to the administration of settlement schemes, and especially the well-documented and much-visited Mwea Irrigation Settlement north of Nairobi, a honeypot which attracted other researcher bees, or flies, besides myself.[7] Mwea, with its strong disciplinary management, and its agricultural and economic success, was regarded as a model for development and much visited and referred to in policy discussions. However, the seminal much-cited and misquoted research of Jane Hanger and Jon Moris (1973) showed that women were much worse off on the scheme. Settlement schemes were a great subject at the time: they had high political priority, they were much researched, there was a burgeoning grey literature, and comparative analysis and practical lessons were in demand.

Camouflaged by a PhD, I then became a 'lecturer' in the Department of Politics and Sociology in Glasgow for three years. Development studies was not yet a subject at Glasgow. My mentor, Bill Mackenzie, was a wonderfully humane polymath, deeply committed to development in Africa, who gave me freedom to continue research and to write. I never had to give a lecture and did little teaching. I met and married Jenny who did lecture, in psychology. I got into writing and editing, and then moved in 1969 to an Honorary Fellowship at IDS Sussex, then three years old, and an appointment to IDS Nairobi to coordinate evaluation for the Kenyan government's Special Rural Development Programme (SRDP). After that and a spell in Botswana, while still based at (a very tolerant) IDS Sussex, I had two years mainly in Sri Lanka and Tamil Nadu with Barbara and John Harriss and Indian and Sri Lankan colleagues, as assistant director to Benny Farmer doing fieldwork on agrarian change and the lack of a green revolution in rice (Farmer, 1977).

UNHCR and the Ford Foundation

Much of the time when I was physically at IDS is a blur. The periods abroad from IDS stand out more, two in particular. For a year and a half (1975–76), I was the first Evaluation Officer with UNHCR, based in Geneva. This was an organization largely staffed and dominated by lawyers recruited to deal with refugees from Eastern Europe. Their professional training and inclinations were to deal with legal issues. In terms of the breadth of concerns in development and so also in development studies, UNHCR was a sort of coelacanth, a survivor from an earlier, less evolved age. It had no in-house competence in health, education, resettlement or agriculture. At the same time there were millions of rural refugees in Africa. I concentrated on them and tried to bring them to light as people, not just statistics, and to counteract convenient myths that they could be taken care of by African hospitality. Colleagues could not believe that I would leave UNHCR after only 18 months, but by then I had done the main task. And someone had warned me that I was beginning to become like a UN civil servant, which I took as a health warning, since many were such political animals.[8]

Later (1981–84), based in Delhi, I was the last Ford Foundation staff member to be a Project Specialist (meaning someone who works substantively on a subject). As a Programme Officer I was responsible for making and managing grants for irrigation management and social forestry. In this I was singularly unsuccessful, but had tremendous access and opportunities for learning and taking part in professional discussions and debates. These led into thinking and writing about irrigation management, livelihoods, trees, common property resources, rights and access.

Methodology and participation

From the early 1970s methodology became more and more central to what I found myself doing. Questionnaire surveys had proved ponderous, slow and inefficient, even when they were well carried out as by the SRDP in Kenya and rice-related research in South Asia. RRA (rapid rural appraisal) was evolved by practitioners in many places who were seeking more cost-effective alternatives. In the late 1970s there was a workshop and then an international conference on RRA at IDS. In 1985 the international conference on RRA at Khon Kaen in Thailand (KKU, 1987) was a landmark. RRA training and field visits in Ethiopia, Kenya and West Bengal pointed to the potential of group-visual methods. I was then privileged to have two years (1989–91) based in Hyderabad with the Administrative Staff College of India at the time when Indian innovators were evolving PRA (participatory rural appraisal) approaches and methods, and the PRA explosion began. 'Bliss was it in that dawn to be alive', or so it seemed. It is difficult to express the amazement and exhilaration of those days when we discovered that 'they can do it', that poor people, without education, women, children and men, had capacities to map, diagram and analyse of which we had not dreamt. After that I spent most of the 1990s back in IDS, collaborating with the International Institute for Environment and Development (IIED), networking and trying to support the spread of PRA and of good practices, latterly with colleagues in the Participation Group at IDS, who were working across a wider range of subjects including participation in governance, human rights, citizenship, poverty and policy.[9]

Reflections and lessons

Reflections on these experiences relate to what we do and how we do it in development studies. We all have different endowments, opportunities and trajectories. Development studies themselves, radical or not, undergo radical changes. They are, and should be, in constant flux and evolution. They are, and should be, influenced by and influencing the ever-changing external environment of development policy, power, relationships and practice. But development studies are not an external given. They are also populated, animated, influenced and evolved by us individuals who are engaged in them. Our pathways and life experiences are both moulded by and mould development experience and development studies. We are many sorts of people. Some readers will identify themselves also as actual or would-be development nomads. There are still a number of us but we may be an endangered species.

Reflecting on my wanderings, and rationalizing after the fact, I can see four aspects which illuminate and in part explain what happened, and which may point to more general insights and lessons for those of us in development studies: comparative advantage and luck; making mistakes; reversals – standing on one's head (or more prosaically, seeing things differently); and issues of development nomadism and ecosystem change. This last concludes that most of us in development studies options are more constrained by funders than we were.

Comparative advantage and luck

Before drawing lessons, we have to recognize luck. I have been lucky, and luck and coincidence have provided a sort of personal comparative advantage which few others will have. Here is some of my luck, in roughly chronological sequence.

The first was studying the Italian Risorgimento (the unification of Italy) at university. This entailed critical analysis of primary documents, with all their contradictions and even forgeries. It embedded a scepticism about evidence, sources and methods in research that have lasted well, and I learned how knowledge is, as we now say, constructed, fallible and always open to questioning and doubt.

Then I was fortunate in patrons and colleagues. A sequence of patrons were inspiring and enabling, giving me confidence and opportunities, and launching me out. Special among these were Bill Mackenzie at Manchester and Glasgow, Guy Hunter at the East African Staff College, and Benny Farmer at the Centre for South Asian Studies, Cambridge. I can think of no other contemporary who was so privileged. The same goes for my colleagues in fieldwork in Kenya, Sri Lanka and India, who were friends then and have become friends for life. Throughout, my colleagues in IDS blessed me with a benign tolerance. And there were others in other institutions such as IIED, the Overseas Development Institute (ODI) and Wye College, who were congenial co-conspirators with the solidarity of heretics who are a minority.

Another debt is to those who taught me that I did not know how to write. At school I was told, 'Chambers, your sentences are too angular'. Charles Chenevix Trench, my first District Commissioner in Kenya, passed on to me his love of strange and funny events, of whimsical anecdote and of stories told against oneself, which he constantly wrote up for the entertainment of others (e.g. Chenevix Trench, 1964). Here I learned to relish unusual experience, to enjoy writing about it, and above all to laugh at myself and not to take myself too seriously. Charles wrote in my final confidential report, 'He is incurably verbose on paper'. Alan Simmance at the KIA went through one of my texts crossing out about one word in five. Harry Hanson, who examined my thesis, hammered me for a pretentious quotation from Talcott Parsons. After over a year with UNHCR in Geneva I was told that, 'You are beginning to write like a UN civil servant'. I vividly remember these shocks. They startled me into trying to write more clearly and enjoying playing with words and their patterns.

A less obvious piece of luck was not having to lecture. To lecture, you have to read and remember what others have written, reinforcing it then through public repetition. I did not know enough of any relevant subject to be able to give a formal lecture during my three years at Glasgow, and am amazed to realize that I have only ever given one in 35 years at the University of Sussex. Instead I have taken the easier option of participatory workshops, trying, but not always succeeding, to do something new each time. Optimal unpreparedness and trying to facilitate more open-ended participatory learning in place of more closed didactic teaching have helped. But lack of time and energy, laziness, and finding exercises and sequences which seem to work, have lured me into repetition. In consequence I have deceived myself, constructing through speech and public performance false beliefs, progressively discarding caveats and fitting what I say to the needs of the occasion. I do not think many lecturers realize that giving a lecture again and again is, like a catechism, disabling and conservative, because each time we say something we embed it, remember it better and believe it more, diminishing our doubts, finding it easier to repeat, and to a degree closing our minds.

Yet another comparative advantage came from an interstitial existence between disciplines. This meant that I did not need to master or meddle in dominant development studies debates. Once I asked John Harriss whether I should make the effort to understand the mode of production controversies which were raging not least in the pages of *Economic and Political Weekly*. I have since applied his advice that it would not be worth my while to study other transient turbulences in the academic mainstream, complacently assuring myself that I was adhering to the principle of optimal ignorance. There was after all plenty else to do that was more exciting and less demanding.

The most significant and decisive lessons have come from failure and humiliation. When it became clear with the SRDP evaluation in Kenya that I was a hopeless manager, I ran away to consultancies, research and writing, and remained free from having to manage anything substantial for the rest of my life.[10] Later, being turned down for a chair by the IDS appointments board was a brilliant reinforcement and confirmation: it liberated me from posing as an academic, and the humiliation and hurt became a driving force of anger and energy.

The most important condition of all was security and freedom: a fellowship at IDS provided a stable base and an organization and colleagues who tolerated and even encouraged my physical and intellectual nomadism. In development studies, the like of this no longer exists. IDS was a good place to be in, leave and then return to. More than merely a dry-season reserve pasture, it had a reputation, convening power, and through its core funding, flexibility. Much of this was in the days when reappointment was reasonably safe if you wrote a book every five years or so and contributed something to courses when you were around. It was a busy and challenging place, and work was hard. But I was free to go on secondment to other jobs, and also to explore. There was a precious, glorious freedom to spend time in other countries, and to move from topic to topic (see also below).

So it was that much of my comparative advantage came from not having to lecture, not having administrative responsibility, not being promoted, not having research projects to run, and not having to invest time, as many do now, in the often demoralizing business of preparing competitive bids.

Making mistakes

I have often been wrong and have made many mistakes. Four stand out and are common enough to deserve description, as warnings and learning for myself and perhaps for others.

Combining commitment, enthusiasm, educated ignorance and power. These compounded each other with grazing schemes in Samburu District, Kenya. It was arrogant and wrong to try to induce Samburu pastoralists to accept an alien system. The water introduced probably did more harm than good by allowing heavy grazing of areas earlier protected by lack of water. Like other missionaries blinded by their belief in themselves, I was wrong to think that meaning well was enough. Later I have come to understand how as a district officer I was doubly disabled: by 'education' and by power. The education – a 'good' degree in history at a 'good' university – led me to think I knew when I did not know; power as an administrator (executive and judiciary in the same person) reinforced the disability by reducing the need to compromise or adapt to others. I am astonished by the arbitrary decisiveness of some of the things I did. The collapse of grazing schemes in Samburu was a salutary slap in the face. It symbolized failure of a mindset, behaviours and attitudes and demanded critical examination both of the system (which was transforming anyway with Independence) and of myself. There are questions here for those development professionals with power in aid agencies, governments, NGOs, university departments, research institutes and consultancies.

Accepting conventional methodology as a given. I was slow to question questionnaires. In Kenya I passionately advocated repeating a survey with a control area to identify the impacts of the Zaina Gravity Reticulated Water Scheme, but any results would have been useless. In the South Asian work I was slow to realize how much better it would have been to use local categories, for example for soil types, instead of composing a questionnaire in Cambridge. It took me too long to see the need to challenge methodology and to have the courage to do so. The lesson (see below) is to strive for self-critical epistemological awareness and to seek new ways of doing things.

Imposing a managerial mindset. This manifested in studying Mwea and writing it up. Jon Moris pointed out to me that on every point of contention between the management and the settlers – and there were many – I took the management's point of view. It took me years to recognize and offset this hangover from my days as an administrator and decolonize my mind. Yet later when studying canal irrigation management in South Asia, this same top-down orientation still predisposed me to a managerial solution for bad distribution of water on canal systems: discipline was to be tightened among the staff who controlled and distributed water. Mick Moore disagreed. Subsequent experience showed that the solution was not top-down discipline as I advocated but bottom-up participation empowering of groups of irrigators. The lesson is introspection to understand and offset the way life's experiences predispose us to interpretations, conclusions and recommendations.

Being out of date. After my time with the Ford Foundation in India (1981–83) I sat down to write about canal irrigation management. My material and mindset was mainly from the 1970s. But irrigation was moving on. In the mid-1980s, while I was writing the book (published only in 1988!), two new topics were coming to the top of the agenda: financing irrigation, previously heavily subsidized; and farmer participation. But the book was already too long, I was no longer able to update it in the field, and I badly wanted to get it out of the way and move on. This was a cost of nomadism. It is also a warning about the costs of long gestation for books based on empirical data – the danger of being out of touch, late and out of date by the time they are published. The lessons are to strive to write, publish and share with little delay (fortunately now with the web much easier than it was); and to be ruthless with oneself in rewriting and updating rapidly before publication.[11]

In sum, the lessons are personal: to be critically self-reflective, alert and aware, and ever willing to question and to change.

Reversals: standing on one's head

Reversals was the word which summed up the changes taking place in the 1980s and 90s both in development orientations and in my own life. Polarizations and dichotomies, paired lists of contrasts, comparing normal professionalism and a new professionalism which expressed the reversals, coming to see the contrasts as between a paradigm of things and a paradigm of people – unsubtle and stark though these oppositions were, they served to summarize the paradigmatic contrasts and tensions which many were perceiving and experiencing. As the verses celebrating Hans Singer's 75th birthday had it:

'You are old, Father William,' the young man said,
'And your hair has become very white;
And yet you incessantly stand on your head –
Do you think, at your age, it is right?'

Alice's Adventures in Wonderland, Lewis Carroll

And

Normal professionals face the core
And turn their backs upon the poor;
New ones by standing on their head
Face the periphery instead.

(Clay and Shaw, 1987: 229 and 253)

As more and more development professionals 'stood on their heads', things came to be seen differently. In many fields, reversals and professional transformations began or continued and gathered momentum and even respectability.

Transforming reversals occurred, for example, in agricultural science and knowledge. Robert Rhoades' *The Art of the Informal Agricultural Survey* (1982) stressed changes in behaviour of researchers with farmers, and Paul Richards' *Indigenous Agricultural Revolution* (1985) demonstrated in detail the value and validities of indigenous technical knowledge. Both were landmarks, widely influential and revolutionary in their implications. Not just the knowledge but the experimental abilities of farmers were increasingly recognized. Jacqui Ashby's International Centre for Tropical Agriculture (CIAT) video *The IPRA Method*, and Michel Pimbert and P.V. Satheesh's International Crops Research Institute for the Semi-arid Tropics (ICRISAT, 1991) video *Participatory Research with Women Farmers* had a huge impact in the 1990s. In the mid-2000s we have moved so far that in international agricultural research institutes it is now common for farmers to be involved not just in evaluating varieties, but in the whole breeding process, including selecting the original crosses, a degree of participation unthinkable in the 1980s. Beyond this, in the 2000s there is a new critical awareness of research process and relationships with the emergence in the Consultative Group for International Agricultural Research (CGIAR) system of the theme of Institutional Learning and Change (Watts et al., 2003),[12] reflecting back critically on the system itself.

Reversals of behaviours and relationships and transformations of mindsets went together. With much that changed, practice came first and theory later. One part of this was the explosion of innovation with PRA (originally Participatory Rural Appraisal, now sometimes Participation, Reflection and

Action, or simply PRA), where outsiders changed their behaviour and became the facilitators and local people the analysts, expressing their own realities. The epicentres of innovation were in countries of the South, especially in South Asia and sub-Saharan Africa. In the 1990s many university faculty members in the South and North were left standing, while students asked to be taught and to use the new visual and group approaches and methods, and the behaviours and attitudes which they demanded. Development studies courses and university departments lagged behind field practice and when they did begin to adopt the new approaches and methods their understanding and teaching was often flawed, suffering from the inexperience of university faculty. Practitioners from the South were at times appalled by the ignorance of teachers in the North. Abuses have now diminished and practice has improved as the significance of behaviour, attitudes and relationships has gradually sunk in. Generally, more participatory approaches to teaching and learning in development courses have been evolved[13] and are spreading (Taylor and Fransman, 2003).

Nomadism and ecosystem change

To be geographically, institutionally and intellectually nomadic seems to require two conditions: emerging gaps or patches to graze or cultivate; and funding and freedom.

It was good fortune that gaps were there to be found and explored: methods for rapid appraisal, canal irrigation management, tropical seasonality, trees as savings, water and poor people, micro-environments unobserved, farmer-first approaches in agricultural research and extension, vulnerability as a dimension of deprivation, sustainable livelihoods, and so on. Today, change in many dimensions seems to be accelerating, which should mean that new issues and gaps, and the opportunities and needs they present, will continue to open up for us all.

But funding and freedom are more the problem now. Organizations need funds to create posts and people need security and opportunities to move around. IDS was privileged, and the envy of others, with its core funding in the 1970s and 1980s. It allowed freedom not only for longer-term work but also for rapid opportunism and leaping on serendipitous leads. Here is an example. In the late 1970s someone remarked in a seminar that they had found births peaking during the monsoon in Bangladesh. Richard Longhurst, just back from fieldwork said he had found the same during the rains in Northern Nigeria. So we asked – why? At once we were into the rich and wonderfully complex subject of seasonality. Richard and I wrote a two-page note and were allocated £10,000 from the IDS budget for a conference on tropical seasonality and poverty, a subject as enthralling as it was neglected and important, and a book resulted. Today, we are so projectized and log-framed that we would lack the flexibility to open up a subject like that. It does not fit in any box. We would face negotiation, hassle, delay, uncertainty and worry, wondering how we were going to earn our way while we took the risks of making a proposal that had not been asked for. Seasonality remains a Cinderella in development: vital, pervasive, enormously significant for many poor people, cross-cutting disciplines, and still systemically underperceived by professionals at huge cost in stress, suffering and impoverishment to hundreds of millions of poor people.[14] Yet it is hard to imagine funding now to support work on tropical seasonality as a general subject.

Research agendas in the 2000s appear to be determined more by funders than they were. Core funds are scarcer and scarcer. There is less trust, more targets, less flexibility, more 'accountability' upwards to where the money comes from. I am vulnerable to the fantasy of a past golden age. Yet even allowing for that, it seems to me that development studies now suffer from too much centralized decision-making linked to funding, with a loss of nimble opportunism. Do we not need more nomadism and more nomads? If so, what are the implications for those who fund development studies?

A radical agenda for future development studies?

Qualifications, caveats and context

In some circles, to be radical, or to label oneself as radical, is approved and politically correct. There can then be a danger of posturing as radical for radical's sake. In development studies, I believe there is a case for persisting with and continuing to evolve many of the good things which are already being done, some of them bequeathed by yesterday's radicalism, no longer very new, but with far still to go: concerns, for example, with gender relations, participation and sustainability. There is a case, too, for continuity of in-depth research. What is radical can also rotate; some cutting edges move in circles. This can mean, for example, reviving and reinforcing the orientations and concerns with redistribution and equity from the 1970s.

It is also important to recognize that over the 1980s and 1990s, in the UK at least, much has changed for the better. First, dissemination used to be a blind spot: on ESCOR[15] in the 1970s it was again and again necessary to argue to *raise* the budgets of research projects to include provision for workshops, publications and other forms of dissemination. That has now been corrected. Second, international collaboration and South–South and South–North links are more common, and relationships more collegial. Long past are the days when the South came to the North mainly to be trained: learning now is reciprocal, and flows of innovation and learning are increasingly from South to North. Third, in the UK priority subjects are more systematically opened up jointly with institutions in the South through the Development Research Centres, for example Chronic Poverty at Manchester, and Citizenship, Participation and Accountability at IDS. Finally, the agenda does move, and quite rapidly. Recent examples on the social side alone are human rights, violence, conflict, disability, chronic poverty, poor people's concepts of ill-being and well-being, and dimensions of power and relationships (e.g. Groves and Hinton, 2004). And each discipline and sector has its own evolving agenda.

A case can also be made for a historical view and learning from the past. Rediscovering wheels has its value in learning for oneself. Unfortunately, though, much learning is expensive and unnecessary because old lessons have been lost. Community-Driven Development driven by the World Bank and participatory natural resource management driven by national bureaucracies are relearning the costly but forgotten lessons of Community Development in the 1950s and 1960s. Here, as elsewhere, one can ask whether the experience of the past has been studied enough and the lessons presented to those who make policy today.

All that said, immobility, inertia and conservatism give grounds for concern. I sense that there is less inclination and opportunity for development professionals to change types of jobs and organizations and that fewer people do it. I have no supporting statistics, and I hope I am wrong. To be sure, there are still people who move in and out of NGOs, aid agencies, and research and academic institutions, but they appear a minority. In the UK in the 1960s and 70s, development studies was a growth industry: new institutes and centres were being founded. But now in the 2000s the security of an expanding job market has passed, and I think more people stay on in their posts rather than risk a transition. In IDS in the 1970s and into the 1980s, Fellows were *expected* on average to spend a third of their time on spells abroad, funded from other sources. So it was that I could work on evaluation in the IDS Nairobi, on rice-related field research in South Asia, on rural refugees with UNHCR in Geneva and Africa, on irrigation and social forestry with the Ford Foundation in Delhi, and on PRA with the Administrative Staff College of India. Today there seems less latitude for such spells abroad, which for me were so challenging, energizing and formative; and that is a loss.

There is, of course, a case for specialization, by subject, by country or by region. There is a case for spending time in one organization or place. But specialization and isolation have been responsible for many of the worst errors in development policy and practice. To offset these requires that development studies be polymath, grounded in and continually keeping up to date with micro and macro realities, and theoretically informed yet open to an eclectic pluralism. Loss of mobility, with careers limited to one organization and one place, whatever their benefits, has costs in the range of experiences and learning forgone.

A radical reconfiguration?

There will be many views about what might be a radical agenda for future development studies. The reader may wish to make a personal list before reading mine. What follows draws on current ideas and insights from colleagues, and is where my journey as a nomad has brought me. There is much, much else besides what follows here.

Radicalism often refers to analysis, advocacy and action for major social change. What follows in no way negates such activities. But there is a complementary critical radicalism which introduces and explores new dimensions and activities which cross-cut subjects and contexts. These dimensions and activities are little recognized, attract few funds, and are not represented by any one discipline or profession, or if they are, not by one that is prominent in development studies. These dimensions and activities overlap and interact. Those I shall outline are: methodology, critical reflexivity, agency and the personal dimension, power and relationships, and pedagogy for the powerful, all combining to become a critical reconfiguration.

Methodology refers to the ways we do things and their patterns. Methodology is implicit in every development studies activity – research, teaching, learning, convening, networking, writing, conferences and so on. There is also the metasubject of how methodologies can be developed.[16] This is even more neglected. In participatory research, however, experience has been that each topic and context needs the invention, piloting and refining of its own tailor-made methodology.[17] Despite this experience, though, methodology is still a relatively neglected subject in development studies. Habits persist: in fieldwork, bad questionnaire surveys survive. There are brilliant examples of RRA and PRA, but quality and ethics are often problematic. Significant innovations are overlooked: in the mainstream little interest has been shown in participatory approaches and methods for generating statistics.[18,19] How things are done and can or could be done is an issue across subjects and topics, not just those well established in disciplinary mainstreams, but also in others such as bureaucratic procedures, participatory poverty assessments, accountabilities upwards and downwards, natural resource management, advocacy, training for new concerns such as human rights, work on HIV/AIDS, chronic poverty, and many more. One methodology we need is to know better how to analyse the links between our choices, acts of commission and omission, and those who are meant to benefit, and so to learn to make better decisions about what to do.

Critical reflexivity refers to reflecting critically on oneself. The academic debates of development studies have been weak on transparent reflexivity. Willingness to examine and present personal predispositions seems inversely related to the conviction, passion and rigidity with which views are held and taught. This is independent of right or left, and largely independent of discipline. It was there as much with some of the old-style Marxists of the 1960s and 1970s as with some of the neoliberal marketeers of the 1990s and 2000s. It is a matter not just of the inherent validity of an ideology or world view but also of personality and personal orientation. This is not at all to say that the Marxists or the neoliberals were or are all wrong. It is, rather, to say that it would be easier for us all to get closer to useful understanding and good ideas about what can and should be done, and for others to form sound judgements about their views, if they could examine and be transparent about their life experiences, conditioning, and the predispositions to which these have given rise.

Development studies especially need self-critical *epistemological* awareness – that is, being critically aware of how knowledge is formed by the interplay of what is outside, and what is inside, ourselves. Outside ourselves, this concerns being aware not just of methodology but also of the external processes of observation and interaction which inform us; and inside ourselves, this concerns trying to be aware of our own predispositions to select, interpret and frame. This makes doubt a virtue, and being able to say, 'I don't know' and 'I was wrong'. It can lead to modifying how we seek to learn, changing the approaches and methodologies we use, trying to understand and offset our mindsets and orientations, and being more sensitive to and aware of the realities of others.

Agency and the personal dimension follow on. This is so self-evident that it is embarrassing even to make the point. But what happens in development results largely from human action, from the choices and actions of actors. For many actors in development studies, making a difference is a major, if not the major, motivation. Yet, and again strangely, there is little systematic analysis of the causal links between our work – that book, that conference, that idea – and the poor, deprived, vulnerable and excluded people whom we seek to serve. There is little analysis of career trajectories and life experiences, or of the best balance between specialization and nomadism, between working in one sort of organization and in several. Unsurprisingly, I would argue we need more semi-nomadic, perhaps transhumant, professionals who move around and gain experience in different contexts, countries and organizations. In North and South alike, this would mean more people who had spent different parts of their lives in other countries, in aid bureaucracies, NGOs and research institutes, who had done grassroots fieldwork, and who could bring to their work, in whatever context, a kaleidoscope of experience. To do this is harder than it was but it needs to be encouraged and made easier.

Power and relationships have only recently become a major focus of attention. Power in political science has a long genealogy. But power in relationships between development actors has received little attention. In their edited book *Inclusive Aid: Power and Relationships in International Development* (2004) Leslie Groves and Rachel Hinton have placed it firmly on the agenda, with the challenge to change behaviour, attitudes and mindsets, and procedures, principles and conditionalities, to make real the rhetoric of partnership, empowerment, ownership, participation, accountability and transparency.[20]

Pedagogy for the powerful. Methodology, reflexivity, agency and making a difference, and power and relationships converge and overlap, and together with parts of my life experience point to the need for a pedagogy for the powerful or (with apologies to Paulo Freire, though I hope he would have approved) for the oppressors, or more tactfully, the non-oppressed. My power, ignorance and ignorance of my ignorance as a district officer led me to do harm when I meant to do good and thought I was doing good. In the history of development there are many good things, but the avoidable errors are appalling. Tens, perhaps hundreds, of millions of poor people were deprived, suffered and often died as a result of policies of structural adjustment alone. We need better ways, procedures, methodologies and experiences to enable those who make and influence policy, and ourselves in development studies, to be more aware, to get it right, and to do better. The big priority now is realism, to bridge and close the chasm which has opened even wider between the incestuous love–hate relationships of lenders, donors and policy-makers in their capital city and five-star hotel meetings and workshops, and the poor people for whose benefit our development industry is said to exist. Recognizing their power in development studies, we can ask too whether we need a pedagogy for funders.

There is no magic wand, no one solution. But one process shows promise of practicality and impact. It is the immersion.[21,22] In this, outsiders – policy-makers, powerful people, development professionals of all sorts including academics – have the opportunity to spend a few days hosted by a poor family or community, sharing some of their life, helping them in their daily tasks, learning their life histories, and seeing things from their, peripheral, perspective. Pioneered by Karl Osner in the 1980s, used by the World Bank for senior managers and others since the mid-1990s, and now spreading to other agencies and organizations, immersions have shown the potential to make a radical difference to those who can make a radical difference. When I reflect on my own past in development and development studies, and my errors and failures of understanding, I can speculate on how differently (and better) I would have acted had I had the experience of participatory research and regular immersions.

A radical reconfiguration of development studies would then include more individual reflexivity, especially self-critical epistemological awareness, and deliberate efforts, through practices like immersions, to gain the experiential learning of reversals. It would pay more attention to methodology. It would entail more conscious actions to support some nomadism, and to avoid the traps of isolation, insulation and complacency to which we are so vulnerable, especially, but not only, those of us in and from the North. Above all, it would recognize the importance of policy-makers, the wealthy and others with power, and make it a priority to learn about how they, as well as ourselves, can change and act more for the better. For they are the biggest blind spot in development studies. If we are serious about poverty, we have to be serious about powerful people as people.

Acknowledgement

This chapter was written at the invitation of Uma Kothari for a conference on 'A Radical History of Development Studies' held in November 2002 at the Institute for Development Policy and Management at the University of

Manchester, and published in her book (Kothari, 2005: 67–87). I am grateful to Uma Kothari for constructively critical reflections on drafts of this chapter.

Notes

1. There are markers of ageing. One is the first time you are, if thin, described as 'sprightly'. Another, which I recently passed, is when you are introduced as having 'spent a lifetime …'.
2. This is not the place for detail on subjects such as relationships with parents, childhood traumas, early toilet training and the like, although we know these have a profound effect on us. To recount these would not, I think, significantly illuminate what follows.
3. Another form of optimist, perhaps more common in our credit-for-consumption Northern world than before, drains the half-full glass and asks for more.
4. I suspect that there was a security file on me dating back to wild days during National Service and carrying the motion: 'This House welcomes the advent of communism in China'. This was at the time of the Korean War. In my interview for HMOCS I was probed for my reasons, perhaps political or ideological, for wanting to go to Kenya, a 'difficult' colony with minority problems. It ended happily enough with, 'Oh my dear chap, if you want to go to Kenya for the *mountains* …' and I was through.
5. As teaching material I requested the British Council to send us two books: Isaiah Berlin on Karl Marx; and *Mein Kampf*. The response was that these could not be supplied because of their political nature. Perhaps someone feared a parliamentary question: 'Is the Minister aware that the British Council in Kenya is supplying …?'. We asked for Lord Lugard's Diaries instead. These were deemed acceptable.
6. The East African Staff College had headquarters in Nairobi in what are now the income tax offices. It subsequently grew in size and scope, and has become ESAMI (The Eastern and Southern Africa Management Institute) with a multi-storey building in Arusha, Tanzania.
7. So many researchers descended on Mwea that Jon Moris and I were able to edit a book on the scheme (Chambers and Moris, 1973).
8. Before I joined it UNHCR was described to me as a 'panier de crabes' (a basket of crabs).
9. Subsequently I have become increasingly involved with another participatory methodology – community-led total sanitation, for which see www.communityledtotalsanitation.org.
10. I have to qualify this. In the 1990s at IDS I found myself managing a substantial budget but was immensely fortunate that before it got completely out of hand John Gaventa came and took over.
11. I smile at my hypocrisy in writing this. I have a book which has been with the publisher for nearly three months during which much has happened. Instead of updating it urgently, I am trying to complete this chapter to meet its third deadline. The kindest gloss I can give this is that there are always trade-offs.

12. This paper symbolizes the scope for reversals and the vicissitudes of development: the authors' names are in reverse alphabetical order; and within months the International Service for National Agricultural Research which published the paper had ceased to exist.
13. For example an innovative MA in Participation, Social Change and Development was launched by IDS and the University of Sussex in 2004.
14. A recent manifestation of the neglect of the multiple interlocking dimensions of seasonal deprivation for poor people is an artefact of the top-down, insulated, centre-outwards analysis that informs efforts to achieve the Millennium Development Goals. Perhaps this is only to be expected from season-proofed mainly Northern professionals.
15. The Economic and Social Council for Research, which advised on government grants for economic and social development research.
16. See for instance Brock and Pettit, 2007.
17. See Cromwell et al., 2001 and Barahona and Levy, 2003 for examples from Malawi. Many professionals persist in thinking that they can take participatory methodologies off the shelf, as though they were questionnaires.
18. However, the Statistical Services Centre at Reading University did substantial work in this area. See, for example, Barahona and Levy, 2003.
19. In 2013 there is more interest. There have been more and more innovations. See Holland, 2013.
20. There is now (2013) a considerable literature. See VeneKlasen and Miller, 2002; Eyben et al., 2006 for an IDS Bulletin and John Gaventa at www. powercube.net
21. For an overview and sources see Eyben, 2004; for fuller analysis and distillations of experience, Irvine et al., 2004; for an example and outcomes, Chen et al., 2004; for practical guidelines, Osner, 2004; and for a participatory research variant, Jupp, 2004.
22. For accounts and analysis of immersion experiences see Birch and Catani, 2007.

CHAPTER 2

Power, knowledge and policy influence: reflections on an experience[1]

From 1998 through 2000 from my base at IDS I collaborated with a team in the World Bank which managed a study in 23 countries to elicit the voices and realities of poor people to feed into the World Development Report 2000/01 Attacking Poverty. *Critical reflections explore some of the many challenges and decisions faced, among them: whether to engage in the first place; how to optimize practical trade-offs of time, resources, volume of data, and open-endedness versus analysability; dilemmas and decisions in analysis; tensions between professionalism, presentation and policy influence; compromises with mindsets, sound bites of disembodied voices, pressures for messages. Practical lessons are drawn for optimizing through trade-offs, balances and win-wins. The conclusion stresses the pervasive significance of power in forming and framing knowledge, and the case for critical reflexivity and methodological pluralism.*

Keywords: conflicting values, ethics, knowledge and power, outrage, policy influence, poverty, qualitative research, reflexivity, representation, trade-offs

> Poverty is the central issue of our time ... Don't underestimate the importance of confirming within the World Bank that poverty is the central issue ... [Voices of the Poor is] extraordinarily important to me and to the Bank ... extraordinarily important to us in terms of direction ... I need the voices you are unleashing ... Hold me accountable for seeing this through the system ... The first thing we have to do is move our institution ... [I am] looking for an army to help me. If you will become part of that army I will be delighted ... Be constructively critical ... I am willing to make my time available to this group. You need to raise your voices ... [This is] a straightforward offer. It is what I am here to do. I am not here to preside over the status quo.
>
> From remarks by James Wolfensohn, President of the World Bank,
> to the Consultations with the Poor Workshop,
> World Bank, Washington, DC, 22 September 1999

This chapter reflects on personal experience of research, analysis and representation designed to influence policy and practice. The 23-country participatory Consultations with the Poor[2] project was managed from the World Bank and undertaken to influence the *World Development Report 2000/01*. This study illuminates methodological, epistemological and ethical

http://dx.doi.org/10.3362/9781780448220.002

challenges, dilemmas and trade-offs which are common to much policy-oriented research. In the Consultations these were sharpened by the aim to privilege and represent the voices and realities of poor people, consulted on a large scale and in a short time. Researchers had power to determine how open or closed the process was. Knowledge was formed iteratively through interactions of researchers' and participants' priorities, concepts, frames, realities and patterns of analysis and representation. Academic values and practices in part conflicted with the ethics of policy influence. The findings of the Consultations had power to outrage and inspire. Practical lessons can be drawn from the experience and impact of the study.

In this chapter I seek to draw practical lessons concerning power, knowledge and policy influence. It is based on personal reflection on a process and an experience, relating these to a wider body of ideas and evidence. This includes some of my own motivations and limitations, and trade-offs between conflicting values. Much of the material is what I recollect of my behaviour, and the method is critical reflection, embracing error more than celebrating success. I do not pretend to give a balanced overview. Those who criticize qualitative research will find grist to their mill. My challenge to them is to also recognize its strengths, and to be at least equally self-critical and transparent about their own methods and work. It is tempting to quote the Bible and say, 'whoever is without sin cast the first stone'. But that is not entirely appropriate. Let stones be cast, but after beating one's own breast with them first.

In fairness to the co-authors of *Voices of the Poor: Crying Out for Change* – Deepa Narayan, Meera K. Shah, and Patti Petesch – I wish to place on record that I know from personal communications how much more systematic they were than I was. This is an autocritique, not a critique of my colleagues. I shall conclude that a good way forward is a combination of critical reflection, action to offset distortions arising from power relations, and methodological pluralism. I hope these reflections will be of interest and help to others.

Consultations with the Poor

Consultations with the Poor (hereafter the Consultations) was a 23-country study, part of a project known as Voices of the Poor (Narayan et al., 2000b). The intention was to contribute to the concepts and content of the *World Development Report* (WDR) *2000/01 Attacking Poverty*. Apart from the section on impact below, which considers the Voices of the Poor as a whole, this chapter is concerned with the Consultations.

By any standards, the training, fieldwork and initial analysis and synthesis in-country of the Consultations were a considerable practical, logistical and methodological effort.[3] In a few months in late 1998 and very early 1999 two methodological workshops were held, methods pilot-tested in four countries, and a process guide devised. In the first half of 1999, country teams were found and trained; broadly comparable participatory methods of analysis, both verbal and visual, were facilitated with groups of women, men, youths and sometimes children on some 272[4] sites in 23 countries; site reports were written; national workshops were held; 21 national synthesis reports were completed; and an international synthesis workshop was held near Delhi. A Global Synthesis (Narayan et al., 1999) and 21 National Synthesis Reports were published and presented at the World Bank in September, and a final fuller analysis and synthesis appeared as a book, *Voices of the Poor: Crying Out for Change* (Narayan et al., 2000b), a year later.[5]

The process of the Consultations was managed and led within the World Bank. The Participation Group at the IDS at the University of Sussex, UK, was contracted separately by DFID to contribute technical assistance.[6] My own part was to engage on behalf of IDS in the early discussions and negotiations with the World Bank, to take some part in preliminary workshops, and then to be involved in analysis and writing as one of the authors of *Voices of the Poor* (Narayan et al., 2000b).

In the course of this experience I was a participant in the exercise of power in the construction and use of knowledge. This brought home dilemmas and choices involving costs and benefits, trade-offs and a search for win–win solutions in research, analysis and policy influence. It highlighted some ways in which power shapes knowledge. And it pointed to the importance and difficulty of reflexivity. I use reflexivity to mean self-critical epistemological awareness, entailing critical reflection on the part one plays, and one's relationships and interactions play, in the formation, framing and representation of knowledge.

To engage or not to engage

A first choice was whether or not to engage with the Consultations. I was not alone in having reservations about collaborating in research with the World Bank.[7] Previous experience had shown how power, impatience and preconceived ideas and priorities on the part of Bank staff could lead to systemic distortion and deception. I had already written about this as part of the theme that 'all power deceives' (Chambers, 1988: 54–9; 1992; 1997: 71–3, 97–100). I knew of cases where Bank staff had appropriated and taken credit for the work of others, and where Bank staff or editors had infuriated and frustrated researchers by heavily red-pencilling their drafts. I had myself had the title of a paper changed by a Bank editor.[8] There was, too, a sense of a legal bottom line limiting critical comment. I had also had the privilege of being invited to facilitate a workshop at the World Bank on values and incentives in that organization; and what I learnt from that experience did not encourage optimism about early change in its culture and behaviours. At the same time, I had been asking myself deeper questions about the very existence of the Bank, and whether it was or could be on balance a force for good in the world. I may not have been the only person who toyed with the idea of an alternative world development report on poverty and development, to be launched at the same time as the official one.

However, the World Bank, like Everest, is there. It exists. For some the right course may be to criticize and oppose it from outside. For others it is to engage with it, but still from outside. Yet others, including able and committed people whom I know and respect, have joined it to work for change from within. For our part in the Participation Group at IDS, we consulted with colleagues in the South and North. They thought we should engage. At the same time they stressed that the decision was in the end ours.

As incentives to engage, there were the challenges of trying, however modestly, to help develop a new approach to giving voice to poor people on a global scale, and of influencing the World Bank, the WDR and perhaps development thinking, policy and practice more widely. Against engagement was the danger of contributing to the legitimation of the World Bank which might use the exercise for public relations. This might help to cover up its deficiencies and delay recognition of the need for radical change in its staffing, culture, funding and relationships.

In having such a degree of freedom of choice, we were unusually fortunate. For many researchers and consultants, whether in the North or South, choice is more constrained: work commissioned by the World Bank is relatively well paid, raises one's professional status, and may lead to further contracts. Some want the work and income to augment already adequate lifestyles. For them to turn down a contract for ethical reasons ought not to be too problematic. For others – academics and consultants struggling to gain a livelihood, educate their children, care for relatives, and pay a mortgage or build a house – it is harder, though some to their credit do so.[9]

The decision was evenly balanced. The counterfactual is unknowable. The Bank side accepted our amendments to the draft outline for the Consultations project. It also seemed that under the leadership of Ravi Kanbur the WDR 2000/1 would be a major and good step forward in policy thinking. It deserved to be supported and if possible influenced. Within our Participation Group at IDS there was a range of views. However, our core funding from DFID, SDC and Sida, and DFID's willingness to fund us directly for work on the Consultations, seemed to promise a relationship with the Bank of partnership rather than what I had observed in some other cases of funding patron and client. The assurance of independent funding was a factor in tipping the balance. So some of us did engage.

Dilemmas in practical trade-offs

From the start it was clear that with the usual constraints of time and resources there would have to be painful trade-offs. Some of the more challenging and interesting concerned time, resources, scale, representativeness, methods and follow-up. In brief, these were as follows:

Time and resources versus scale and representativeness

There was a tension between paradigms: the dominant statistical canons of validity and those of qualitative research. The former argued for more and the latter for fewer countries, communities and groups of poor people. At an early stage the proposal being explored was for a focused comparable study of possibly 15–20 communities, rural and urban, in each of 30 countries. The latter favoured a smaller number of communities and countries bearing in mind issues of logistics, finance, quality, feasibility of analysis and follow-up with communities: a range of 5–12 countries was discussed. As one who favoured fewer countries and fewer sites, I underestimated the ability of those in the World Bank to make things happen quickly on a large scale. It was remarkable that in the event, 23 countries were involved, with some 272 communities. The opportunism of running with those countries where there was interest, willingness and capacity was a practical trade-off between feasibility and other constraints. There were obvious gaps, but the final tally of countries gave a better spread of representation than might have been expected:

- In Latin America and the Caribbean: Argentina, Bolivia, Brazil, Ecuador and Jamaica.
- In Africa: Egypt, Ethiopia, Ghana, Malawi, Nigeria, Somaliland and Zambia.
- In Asia: Bangladesh, India, Indonesia, Sri Lanka, Thailand and Vietnam.
- In Eastern Europe and the former USSR: Bosnia, Bulgaria, the Kyrgyz Republic, Russia and Uzbekistan.

Scale and financial resources, time, training, fieldwork and in-country analysis

The time taken in early negotiations, the amount and timing of funding, and the deadlines for completion constrained the training of field teams and their work. As an observer who did not take part in this phase, my main reflection is that the scale and quality of the work were beyond reasonable expectations, and this largely because of the intense commitment and sacrifices of those involved. More time and money would have been better, but the urgency and pressure brought out the best in many people.

Scale, time, resources and orientation versus community-level follow-up

The combination of a large scale, shortage of time and resources, and the orientation of the study made local-level follow up difficult in most cases. In the practice of PRA[10] and also in participatory poverty assessments (PPAs) a recurrent concern has been that there should be follow-up at community level, or if this is infeasible, that it should be made abundantly clear from the outset. With PRA, a common abuse has been raising and then disappointing local people's expectations.[11] The Process Guide was clear on this point:

> Avoid generating expectations. Another issue to be kept in mind is that of generating any expectations. A consultative process, like the one being adopted by this study (and with the focus on understanding people's

problems and priorities), can create expectation of some sort of benefits in people's minds. It is important to explain clearly at the very outset that this is only a study to understand poor people's perceptions. There are no direct benefits or follow-up to these discussions. However, it is possible that the results from the study could influence national policy, and in turn have a positive impact on the people's lives in an indirect manner. However, whether or when this will happen cannot be predicted. This may have to be reiterated several times during the course of the fieldwork, as it is highly undesirable to generate any false expectations.

(World Bank, 1999: 51)

In the event, there were a variety of practices and forms in which there were some local benefits. In Bolivia, unemployed workers were paid for their time. In Bangladesh where NGOs (ActionAid, Concern and Proshika) themselves funded the Consultations, there was immediate follow-up in at least one community, Khaliajuri, with a housing programme. In Brazil[12] one community leader used multiple copies of the site report to apply pressure for better services. Also on the positive side of the balance, it is quite common for participants in processes of this sort to say that they gain from meeting and talking to one another, from being listened to with empathy and interest, from their shared analysis, and from finding a sense of solidarity. All the same, the ethical issues of taking people's time and of raising their expectations were and remain a worrying concern, not just in this research but in poverty research generally, whether participatory or not.

Scale, number of aspects and open-endedness versus analysability

From the beginning, we all recognized that the larger the scale, the more the aspects covered and the greater the open-endedness, the more difficult would be the analysis. This was addressed in part by reducing the number of sites in each country to a norm of some 8 to 10; in part by restricting the core topics to four (see below); and in part by a degree of standardization of method. An early proposal that the process should include a questionnaire survey was abandoned. The open-ended and participatory process adopted instead was intended to allow poor people's concerns and categories to emerge from their own experience and analysis.[13] There were still dilemmas of language. Closed categories and narrow concepts would impose 'our' realities on 'theirs'. The Process Guide, moreover, had to be written in English (but was translated into Amharic, Bulgarian, Indonesian, Russian and Spanish).

Power to open and close

Limited time and resources accentuated dilemmas over how much to open or close the participatory processes. As in all research, planning the methodology entailed the exercise of power to set boundaries on what would be found.

In our planning workshops we were acutely aware of these issues, and took pains to choose and recommend participatory approaches, methods and behaviour which would offset biases and limit the extent to which research design determined categories and content. But limits had to be set. After much debate, convergence led to closure on four areas on which poor people were to be invited and facilitated to reflect, analyse and share their experience and ideas. These were:

- Well-being and ill-being – their ideas of good and bad quality of life, degrees and categories of well-being and ill-being, and how relative numbers in these groups had changed.
- Problems and priorities, their relative importance, and how they had changed.
- Relationships with institutions – of the State and of civil society including institutions within communities, with rankings, and how these had changed.
- Gender relations, and how these had changed.

In all cases the approach was initially to be open-ended, with naming and listing by participants, rather than categories suggested by facilitators. There were, though, topics and aspects which were felt to be so important that they should be specified, both to ensure inclusion and to enhance comparability and ease of analysis. The text in the Process Guide concerning well-being and ill-being can illustrate this: first the process was to be more open-ended to enable people to express their own words and values, and then to be more specified in terms formulated for the researchers:

> How do people define well-being or a good quality of life and ill-being or a bad quality of life?… Local definitions of well-being, deprivation, ill being, vulnerability and poverty. Since these terms do not translate easily in local languages, it is better to start by asking the local people for their own terminology and definitions that explain quality of life. Local terminology and definitions must be included in the analysis. Different groups within the same community could be using different terms or phrases for the same subject. (World Bank, 1999: 15–16)

A later section in the Guide was more specific:

> Having discussed people's definition of well-being and poverty/ill-being, we need to introduce some discussion around four pre-determined categories of critical importance to the study. These include:
>
> 1. Risk, security and vulnerability
> 2. Opportunities and social and economic mobility
> 3. Social exclusion
> 4. Social cohesion, crime, conflict and tension
>
> (World Bank, 1999: 15–16)

These had the potential to focus and simplify analysis, as to some extent they did. At the same time, they presented the well-known problems of pre-set categories, and getting out what you put in – compounded by difficulties of translation of terms into local languages.

That said, the researchers' site reports from the communities are a remarkable read. The straitjackets of academic theory, jargon and categories are little in evidence. The reports come over as faithful in reporting the realities and values which poor people presented. They manifest an honesty and vivid realism that shines through and carries conviction.[14]

Synthesis and SOSOTEC

To synthesize so much material generated by participatory processes is not easy. For the national synthesis workshops guidelines were prepared in Washington. For the international synthesis workshop held at Surajkund near Delhi in June 1999, we invented, improvised and drew on experience from elsewhere.[15] We had to minimize obvious dangers like overloading a plenary with presentations of some 20 country reports, failing to capture key insights, and simply reproducing pre-existing categories. We needed also to exploit opportunities. These included enabling country team leaders to share what they felt most significant, collating materials in categories and forms which could be used by the writing team, and benefiting from synergies of discussion and sharing.

Combinations and sequences of the following were used:

- Verbal presentations by team leaders to small groups (based on the experience that we say things we do not write, and often express them more vividly).
- Each member of a small group having responsibility for collecting insights and points on a particular subject and writing these on cards (based on the principle of active listening and active questioning concerning the subjects).
- Members of different groups with the same subject meeting to share what they had harvested (as a means of collating and comparing experiences).
- Card sorting on the ground to encourage rapid and flexible emergence of categories.
- Subject groups setting up stalls or collecting points with their cards and other materials, to which others then added.

Part of this was a day and a half of SOSOTEC (self-organizing systems on the edge of chaos). SOSOTEC describes a family of processes based on minimal rules and a skeleton timetable within which individuals act as they see fit.[16] It presupposes participants with something to share and strong motivation. In the form we used there were collecting points in different rooms for the four main themes of the Consultations. Each theme had one or more coordinator or hunter-gatherer. Scissors, paste, paper and boards were available. Every participant then contributed what and where they could and wanted. Once set up, the system ran itself. Variants of SOSOTEC can be very effective. In the right conditions, under white-heat pressure, participants contribute freely and frankly to a harvest of experience and ideas for a synthesis or report. In the Surajkund workshop we took pains not to constrain contributions simply to the topics of the collecting points. This was done by creating a separate place for reflections and contributions that did not fit the other categories.

Immediately after the Surajkund workshop, the four of us who were to be authors of the book met again and spent a day recording on cards the points of greatest significance that had struck us, organizing these into topics, and then allocating responsibilities between ourselves. This iteration proved useful in giving sharper focus, and bridging between the (considerable) SOSOTEC outputs, which we shared and used, and the next stages of analysis and writing.

Dilemmas and decisions in analysis

The analysis and synthesis of the enormous volume of material – the outputs from the Delhi workshop, many of the 272 site reports which progressively became available, and 21 national synthesis reports – posed huge problems. A book was meant to be in draft by mid-September, giving a mere three months. After the Surajkund workshop, and through most of the summer of 1999, further analysis and synthesis took place both in Washington and at IDS. At IDS, six of us were engaged in parallel, mostly on a part-time basis.[17] In the division of labour with Washington, we were concerned mainly with part of well-being/ill-being and with institutions.

Our method was continuous interaction between the material and categories and subjects that seemed important. We assembled extracts of reports by subject on pinboards. The categories multiplied to accommodate the material, some of it not anticipated. I also started sheets of paper on which we listed evidence and sources for particular issues, such as 'documents and the poor', where these came up or where I felt there might be significant insights. In doing all this we were exercising power in selection and categorization – 'Shall we have a heading for "shelter"?' being a typical question. We tried continuously to select for 'significance' but of course it was unavoidably 'we' who were deciding what was significant. There was, too, a sense of discovery and excitement when something new emerged or was powerfully illustrated.

Meera Shah's approach was more systematic. She read all the site reports for their sections on gender and analysed them, not once, but eventually four times. In this way she evolved and cross-checked categories and insights. This was especially important because of her initially controversial finding, confirmed in a fifth check by research assistants, of a reported overall decline in domestic violence against women (Narayan et al., 2000b: 124–31). In Washington too, a team of full-time research assistants trawled through the material for particular topics, and in some cases wrote synthesizing notes.

In my own work I can identify circularities, self-validations and biases. These were most evident during the deadline pressure of the summer of 1999. These were less than they would have been with the pre-set categories of a questionnaire; and we did try to be aware of them and offset them. Nevertheless they were inescapably there at different stages in the whole process. There are lessons from three in particular: looking for evidence, hidden circularity and mental templates.

Looking for evidence

Ideally, I would have read all the site reports. But this was out of the question. My part-time colleagues trawled through them as they were sent on to us and selected extracts. But even these were too voluminous for synthesis. Moreover it became clear that in order to assess extracts, one needed a fuller context. Forced to compromise, there was an element of 'he that seeketh findeth'. We tried to be open to surprises and new topics and insights. The aim, after all, was to represent the realities of poor people, not to box these into our pre-set categories. There was some success in this. To illustrate, at different stages both those in Washington and those at IDS picked up the following points:

- poor people's negative experiences of the police;
- how small improvements can mean a lot to those who have little;
- the importance of kinship networks, friends and neighbours of the poor;
- the widespread identification of those we described as the 'bottom poor';
- the emergence of the 'new poor' in Eastern Europe and Central Asia;
- cases where poor people said they were better off than they had been.[18]

These emerged strikingly from the evidence.

At the same time there simply was not time to allow everything just to emerge. I felt forced to collect for certain topics. In searching my memory, the clearest example of looking for evidence concerns the importance of the body. On the basis of past experience I believed that the significance of the body as the main asset of many poor people was neglected. This was then a category or concern that I brought to the analysis. I was alert for 'good' quotations or examples that might make or illustrate the theme. They were enough to seem to justify the focus. But I wanted a good summary quotation to make the general point. Somehow I gained the impression that someone in Egypt had said, 'Our bodies are our capital'. This was so apposite that we searched for it again and again. We never found it, and yet I believed it was there. Whether I had imagined what I wanted to hear, or whether perhaps it had been said in a workshop by the Team Leader from Egypt, I simply do not know. Whatever the case, I wanted to find an apt quotation on those lines.

Written like this, a search for evidence to illustrate a theme or a quotation to make a point looks reprehensibly unprofessional. But we can ask whether, unacknowledged, and even without critical awareness, this is not quite common practice. We can ask how frequent such behaviour is, how much it matters, and how it should be treated. Reflective readers will have hints from their own behaviour about how common such search and selection may be. To what extent do we search for and notice what will fit our preconceptions? To what extent do we pick out, remember and repeat words, phrases and quotations which stand out because they either fit our frames of reference, or make points we want to make, or give us material with which to disagree?

That it matters should be beyond dispute. The danger is that it packages realities in conventional forms, excludes discordant evidence, and prevents new understandings. It can be responsible for academic and scientific conservatism, and of serendipity overlooked.

The practical conclusion is to be alert to what one is doing, and especially alert for evidence that does not fit preconceptions. If all one's ideas are confirmed, something is likely to be wrong. A good test may be how many 'ahhas!' there are, how many surprises, how many reorganizations of categories, how many changes of ideas. Those we did have in quite good measure.[19]

Hidden circularity

At one stage in writing we were excited at the emergence of 'places of the poor' as a category. It began as part of the chapter on powerlessness. At the same time, infrastructure – water, roads, housing and other services – came out as a priority of participants which did not fit in the structure of the book. It was an 'ahha!' experience, so obvious with hindsight, when we saw that these two could combine to become a chapter. I allowed myself smug satisfaction that here at least was a category and a set of insights that had been generated freely by poor people's expression of their realities.

Later, I reread the Process Guide on site selection and sampling. Site meant community or neighbourhood, village or urban settlement. I found: 'The sites should be chosen to reflect 2–3 of the most dominant poverty groups in a country'. Then I had a second 'ahha!' moment, jumping to the conclusion that the category was in part an artefact of the methodology, the result of a hidden circularity: if you look for places where poor people are conspicuously concentrated, such as remote villages and urban slums – then of course places of the poor will tend to come out as an organizing idea. But there are other poor people who live in places of the rich and less poor, who would be left out. This, I thought, would make a good example to parade as an insight from self-critical reflection: a category generated by the methodology itself.

A third, more muted and slightly disappointed 'ahha!' moment revealed that it was not so simple. An earlier paragraph in the process guide runs, 'The selection of sites will be influenced by the ongoing processes in a country … In case the study is being linked with an ongoing project, the choice of sites will narrow down to the project area. Similarly, if this study is being linked with another ongoing study in the country, the sites will be chosen from those already selected'. In fact, and sensibly, the basis for selection varied.

My best judgement now is that despite its origins 'places of the poor' is a good organizing concept, justified both analytically and practically: analytically it integrates spatially many interlinked aspects of deprivation; and practically it is a focused source of recommendations for policy.

Mental templates

The process of analysis made me aware of mental templates. These are mentally embedded diagrams into which realities are fitted. Some like Buzan (1974), Waddington (1977) and de Bono (1981) are versatile and use many patterns. Others, like myself, repeatedly use one or a few patterns only. My IDS colleagues were not slow to identify me as a pentaphiliac, a lover of five circles connected with double-headed arrows. I like drawing this pattern. It has a pleasing symmetry. So if there are four or six emergent categories, I try to expand or conflate them to become five. An early symptom of this now chronic personal condition was a deprivation trap (Chambers, 1983: 112), linking physical weakness, poverty, isolation, vulnerability and powerlessness. It just so happened that the last two of these resonated with security and empowerment, which – together with opportunity – were the three main themes of the draft WDR made public in January 1999. This only served to reinforce the pattern. So later, in August of that year, during an intense week in Washington in which our writing team had to organize our tasks, the diagram surfaced again. We kept the structure but changed the content to fit emergent categories and analysis. So the circle of isolation became bad social relations, poverty became material lack and want, and vulnerability became security, while physical weakness and powerlessness remained as they were.

We four authors fitted our division of the work into these categories, each taking one, with powerlessness shared. In the Global Synthesis Summary (Narayan et al., 1999) presented in Washington in September, the diagram represented development as good change, from five circles of ill-being to five of well-being (see Figure 2.1). The central pentagon formed by the doubled-headed connecting lines was characterized as the experience of living and being, of bad and good quality of life.

As analysis proceeded, pentaphilia came under pressure from complexity. In writing about powerlessness the five broke right open and became (temporarily) 12,[20] as a web of multiple dimensions of disadvantage. Many interactions within the writing team led to the version which appeared in the book *Voices of the Poor* (see Figure 2.2).

A practical conclusion is for analysts to be aware of their mental templates, to reflect critically on how they may distort in framing realities, and to expand personal repertoires of analytical diagrams for wider choice and better fit with complexities.

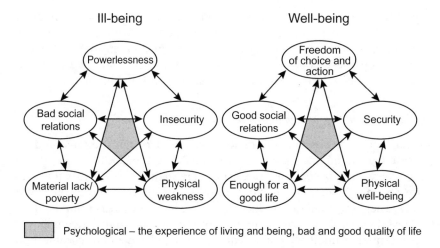

Figure 2.1 Development as good change: from ill-being to well-being

Source: Narayan et al., 1999: 5

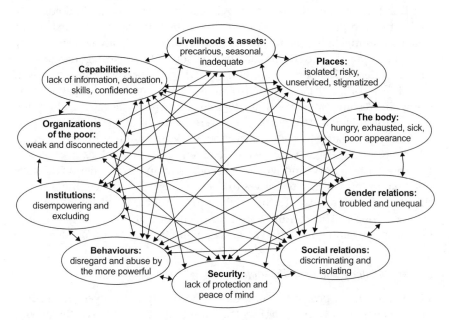

Figure 2.2 Dimensions of powerlessness and ill-being

Source: Narayan et al., 2000b: 249

Professionalism, presentation and policy influence

Among the most thought-provoking trade-offs are those where canons of normal and narrow professional correctness conflict with effectiveness in influencing policy and practice. The values are incommensurable. There is here almost endless scope for casuistry and controversy. Some issues concern numbers, syntax, selecting, editing, summarizing and simplifying.

Numbers: qualitative versus quantitative analysis

We experienced a classic ambivalence over numbers. On the one hand, in policy influence numbers count, and especially in the culture of the World Bank where macro-economists are still king. Statistics carry with them an authority and conviction which qualitative information has been considered to lack. There was therefore an incentive to generate numbers from the data. On the other hand, the nature of much of the data and the large number of sites meant that numbers would require many judgements of classification (which might be questionable or challenged) and would take a lot of time and effort.

There were times when opinion favoured limiting ourselves to qualitative findings only. But there were numbers generated by the processes, and many potentials for counting. I was engaged with the Bangladesh and India field teams briefly at a stage when they were struggling in new territory methodologically to identify and put numbers on trends. This they showed to be possible but time-consuming. Subsequently, all the site reports were analysed centrally by Karen Brock for changes in the top and bottom well-being categories, and for causes and effects of poverty and ill-being. Her numbers were not, however, included in *Voices of the Poor*. Other numerical analysis was undertaken by teams in Washington, notably on two areas of critical debate, again going back to the original site reports. These were trends in domestic violence and institutional rankings by community groups (for the results see Narayan et al., 2000b: 125 and 201–2 respectively). Numerical analysis of data generated through participatory and visual methods remains a frontier with huge potential for providing alternatives to questionnaires, and where the work on the *Voices* process deserves further analysis to contribute to existing experience and techniques.[21] The Consultations confirmed yet again that much work that is participatory and qualitative can generate numbers to inform policy.

Syntax, summary and simplification

Words and syntax pose dilemmas. Care is needed to avoid overgeneralizing. The first chapter of *Voices of the Poor* (Narayan et al., 2000b: 18) concludes with a cautionary discussion of what we felt could and could not be said. We had to avoid expressions like 'everywhere' and 'all over the world'.[22] The evidence from the 272 sites was varied, demanding interpretations that were qualified and nuanced. Through using the terms 'the poor' and 'poor people' we were always in danger of implying misleading homogeneity. Much of what we were discussing could not be reduced accurately to single-sentence or single-phrase generalizations. We resorted to 'often' and its synonyms to convey an appropriately indeterminate degree of significant prevalence.

Pulling in the opposite direction are ethical imperatives for impact. To be remembered, repeated and have an effect, a message is best kept simple and memorable. Through ease of absorption and repetition it may then lead to changed perceptions, priorities, policies and actions.

Much caution is needed here, though, in what is passed on to policymakers and their speechwriters. It is notable how quickly and deeply easily remembered erroneous statistics become embedded in international discourse, and then how difficult they are to dislodge once they have been frequently repeated.[23] Precisely because of the voluminous material and the need to be concise, we were vulnerable to overgeneralizing. Analysing the many site reports for a theme was a formidable task. Nevertheless, for two key issues – trends in domestic violence, and institutional rankings by community groups – the individual site reports were analysed in Washington to derive accurate generalizations. The resulting diagrams (Narayan et al., 2000b: 125 and 201–2) do indeed carry clear but qualified messages, and vindicate the huge effort that went into them.

Shortening and editing were problematic. I found it painful and extraordinarily time-consuming to shorten three chapters by 25 per cent each. Such major shortening presents many agonizing choices of selection and elimination, unavoidably changing the balance and content of what is presented. More problematic still is passing responsibility for further editing to someone who has not been a colleague in the process and who is not familiar with the material. One editor returned a chapter I had drafted and redrafted many times, and then unhappily shortened, after he in turn had further reduced it, with the message that he had cut out the 'emotional' parts.

Sound bite ethics and 'disembodied voices'

Some of the conflicts and dilemmas can be illustrated with a story against myself.

In a draft for this chapter I wrote as follows about James Wolfensohn's speech to the Board of Governors of the World Bank in September 1999:

> Of the poor he said, 'Let me share with you their world in their own words. An old woman in Africa: "A better life for me is to be healthy, peaceful and to live in love without hunger"' (Wolfensohn, 1999).

> Mr Wolfensohn cannot be expected to have known that the Ethiopian woman who said this was reportedly only 26 years old. Nor is he likely to have known that she went on to say, 'Love is more than anything. Money has no value in the absence of love.'

These may, indeed, have been sentiments to which he would have subscribed. But for whatever reason they had been edited out. Nor is such editing so unusual. I have done it myself. When faced with a long quotation, only part of which is relevant to a context, I have shortened it, leaving ellipses to indicate where cuts have been made. For Mr Wolfensohn to have used the whole quotation would have distracted attention from the punchy sequence of voices of the poor he was quoting, and detracted from the impact of his speech. Which arguably was far more important than pedantic faithfulness to the words and meanings of the Ethiopian woman. I wonder what she would think. She might be annoyed, indifferent, flattered, approving or some mix of these. I wonder, too, what you, dear reader, think?

At that stage I knew that in *Voices of the Poor* (Narayan et al., 2000b: 22) the 'full' quotation above appeared at the head of a section 'Wellbeing is multidimensional'. Since I was the main drafter of this section, I accept responsibility for this, and for the form in which it appeared. It was so favourite a quotation that we had debated among us authors where to place it for best effect.

To be on the safe side, however, I sought out the original in the Ethiopia National Synthesis Report (Rahmatu and Kidanu, 1999: 60). This indicated that the woman was a divorcee who had been educated up to grade 9 and then stopped learning because of marriage. I was then dismayed to find the following, as part of a question-and-answer sequence:

> 'What about the future?' 'In the future I have the idea of improving my level of education, go to a town and lead a better life. A better life for me is to be healthy, peaceful and live in love without hunger. Love is more than anything. Money has no value in the absence of love.'
>
> (Rahmatu and Kidanu, 1999)

My first reaction was annoyance: to include the first sentence of her response would weaken the force and impact of my critique. But this was overtaken by a wry smile. For I had caught myself doing precisely what I was criticizing, using an abbreviated quotation, moreover without dotted lines, when the fuller one would not have made my point as effectively.

At issue also is the use of quotations without their full context. On the one hand there were those who considered that 'disembodied voices' could mislead when presented without an understanding of the processes and conditions which led to what was reported to have been said, and even sometimes of what sort of person had been speaking. They could be dismissed as decontextualized anecdotal snippets. On the other hand, there was the thought that a 'good' quotation might make an important point forcefully and contribute to good change. The anecdotal snippet could be an apt illustration.[24]

The issues of syntax, quotation, abbreviation and decontextualizing, and so of disembodying the voices, involve trade-offs between professional and social values which are in part incommensurable. On the one hand there are the professional and academic values of the social scientist who wants to know the context and fuller meaning; on the other there are the values of those who want to make the world a better place for poor people. Professional correctness in adherence to technical and fully qualified accuracy can diminish practical pro-poor effects. The full quotation above would have detracted from the impact of Wolfensohn's speech. The shorter extract was punchy and powerful.

The dilemma is the ethics of the intermediary and of the sound bite. In development practice many of us find ourselves as intermediaries between people and data on the one hand and those with power on the other. There are two big traps. For clarity and contrast these can be caricatured. The first is pedantic and long-winded inclusiveness, heavily and cautiously qualified, sometimes combined with overconsultation. These are more likely to have negative than positive effects: a Provincial Commissioner in Kenya, presented with a big tome of survey findings, exclaimed, 'You expect me to read *this*! And it is only a *draft*!' The trap here is failure to communicate. The second trap is self-regarding selection, shortening, manipulation and even misinterpretation of data to produce simple messages that those in power want to hear and will reward.

The challenge is to find and walk the narrow path between these two. It involves balancing and trade-offs. It demands keen concentration, honest observation and at times courage. The two key questions are: what do the data show? And what can make a change for the better? The answers come in a myriad of decisions, most of them small in appearance and almost invisible. Together they come to make up the representation. The tensions and temptations may be most acute at the interface between those who write speeches and need sound bites and those who supply them with qualified and nuanced information. No easy judgements can be made.

In weighing and balancing these incommensurables, there will be different personal positions. Being trained as a historian, I incline to side with the social anthropologists who want more information, more context, more qualifications, more nuanced interpretations, and strictly keep faith with reported facts. I can also understand, though I may not agree with, the actions of some of those concerned, working under pressure, to achieve pithy relevance to policy. They may justify selecting, shortening and simplifying in order to make a difference for the better. They might argue that all knowledge anyway is socially constructed. In reconstructing knowledge for a good political purpose, they might say, they are expressing a higher value than pedantic faithfulness to earlier constructions of that knowledge.

There is a need here for codes of behaviour. It would help to identify and agree non-tradeables, that is, non-negotiable principles or behaviours. These would provide ethical bedrock to which practitioners could anchor, giving security in the sea of relativism. I shall not try to sketch out such a code: it would best come from a pluralist and participatory process rather than from any one person. There is, though, a meta-level. I would argue that there is an imperative to strive for honest and self-critical epistemological awareness.

This means repeatedly examining how information and knowledge are generated. It means critical straining for honest reflection on how one's own ego, mindset, institutional context, and social and political interests combine to select and shape both personal knowledge and the form it is given when passed on to others.

The power to outrage and inspire

Codes of behaviour demand commitment. For some academics, commitment can be clinically intellectual. For many of those engaged in development, commitment is inspired more by outrage. Even though, to my shame and chagrin, I was unable to take part in the fieldwork, I was shocked and moved by material and evidence from the Consultations. There are moments when one exclaims, 'Hell!' For me and for others, there were many such moments with the Consultations. Their impact on how we see and feel things should not be underestimated.

In any critically reflective review of research, the convention is to conceal what we feel. The vocabulary of disparagement includes 'subjective', 'anecdotal', and worst of all 'emotional'. Saying what shocked and shook me has invited ridicule, and a response on the lines of 'But of course ... we have always known that. ... I am surprised that you are surprised'. Obvious and well known though they may be to others, here are four findings that touched and moved me. Perhaps at some level I knew them in part already. But living and working with the evidence brought them home with a stark sharpness.

1. The weak, hungry and desperate are paid less (Narayan et al., 2000b: 96). A group of men in a fishing community in Malawi were reported to have said: '...we get some K5, buy some maize for one day's consumption; when it is finished we go again ... The problem is that these boat owners know that we are starving. As such we would accept any little wages they would offer to us because they know we are very desperate ... we want to save our children from dying ...' (Khaila et al., 1999: 66).

    Of the 'helpless poor' the Bangladesh National Synthesis Report observed: 'They accept low wage in lean periods. They cannot bargain with the employers given the fact that they will starve without daily wage' (unNabi et al., 1999: 25).

2. Reluctant crime for livelihood (Narayan et al., 2000b: 60–1). The Consultations presented examples of risky livelihoods contrived on or beyond the fringes of legality such as sex work, growing marijuana, drug peddling, selling women and children, and theft. Theft of food appeared extraordinarily widespread, especially in Eastern Europe, the former USSR and rural sub-Saharan Africa. It was described as a risky strategy, undertaken with reluctant desperation. In the reported words of a discussion group participant in Sarajevo: 'Criminality is a result of poverty. When you're hungry, you have to find a way. Hunger doesn't ask' (Lytle, 1999).

3. Police who oppress the poor. I had not realized just how widely and badly the police hurt and hinder poor people, and keep them poor. There were exceptions, outstanding among them the Deputy Superintendent in charge of the Cassava Piece Police Station in Kingston, Jamaica, Rosalie McDonald-Baker, who was warmly praised by a group of poor women. But again and again, the police were experienced as oppressors who persecute the poor and add to the insecurity of their lives and livelihoods. In India they were characterized as 'a licensed evil?' (Praxis, 1999: 35). A group of youngsters in Sacadura Cabral, Brazil, said of the police: 'They hit [first], then they question you ... they get near you and tell you to raise your arms and open your legs. Then they hit your legs. Then they call you shit and demand your documents', (Melo, 1999: 37–8).

4. The bottom poor. Some of the very poorest and worst-off did take part in the Consultations. But often participants identified a group separate from and below themselves as the poorest, variously pitied, feared and looked down upon. The group was diverse, including widows, divorcees, orphans, the chronically sick, very old people, the disabled, the homeless, those without relatives, the mad and mentally disordered, drug addicts, the destitute, and simply those who were very, very poor. A women's group in Malawi identified the 'stunted poor', whose bodies are short and thin and do not shine even after bathing, whose hairs are thin, who have frequent illnesses and who severely lack food (Khaila et al., 1999: 38).

There are many other illustrations in the site reports, in the national synthesis reports, and in *Crying Out for Change*. As with these four, it was not just the finding or reaffirmation that affected me personally. It was also the immediacy of the evidence. The vividness of what poor people were reported to have said vindicated the participatory methodology as means of influencing as well as of learning. Reading about starvation wages, or stealing to feed children, or police brutality, or the bottom poor, is not the same as meeting poor people and hearing about these things directly during fieldwork. Nor are meeting and hearing about them the same as experiencing them personally as one of the victims. But whether through reading, meeting or experiencing, feelings of anger and outrage can be provoked. And feelings like these are drivers for personal commitment to change. They inspire action. The personal impact of disturbing detail can be superficial. It can also be deep. And where powerful people and policy-makers are moved, the links between poor people and policy change are shortened and strengthened (see also McGee, 2002).

Impacts: making a difference?

The ultimate justification for the *Voices of the Poor*, of which the Consultations were a part, has to be net good effects. A balance sheet would be premature. Questions whether, how and how much there has been or will have been a difference for the better or the worse can never be fully answered. Many impacts are invisible. And many are no doubt continuing and still working themselves out. What follow are simply some points that seem worthy of remark.

There were many impacts at personal, community and policy levels. Personally, those poor people who took part were surely affected, as were those who conducted the fieldwork, analysis and synthesis (Adan et al., 2002; Narayan et al., 2000b: 8–16). In some cases there was follow-up at community level, and regional and national policies were influenced (Adan et al., 2002).

The original primary purpose of the Consultations was, however, none of these, but to influence the WDR 2000/2001. The Process Guide expressed it thus: 'The purpose of the Consultations with the Poor study is to enable a wide range of poor people in diverse countries and conditions to share their views in such a way that they can inform and contribute to the concepts and content of the WDR 2000/01' (World Bank, 1999, Introduction).

Influence on the concepts of the WDR is difficult to assess. Its opening sentence, 'Poverty is pronounced deprivation of well-being', and the paragraphs which follow, adding security and empowerment to the definition of well-being, resonate with what came out of the Consultations, as does the stress on the multidimensionality of poverty. The conversion to this broader definition is reflected in the use in the first pages of the WDR of the term 'income poverty' to describe the narrower concept.[25] However, the words security and empowerment were at the core of the WDR draft before the Consultations took place. Possibly, though, the Consultations served to reinforce them in the WDR. The Consultations may also have served to limit any rewriting there may have been in the later stages of preparing the WDR after Ravi Kanbur, the director of the WDR team, had resigned.

Influence on the contents of the WDR is clearer to see. Six of the 91 boxes are derived from the *Voices of the Poor* as a whole, including the first box, which stands out prominently in the Overview. The six are:

1.   The voices of the poor
1.1. Poverty in the voices of poor people
1.4. Measuring voice and power using participatory methods
2.1. On interacting with state institutions: the voices of the poor
5.4. Locked out by health and education fees
6.1. Poor people are often harassed by public officials.

These present some of the most acute and deeply felt concerns expressed by poor participants. There is also a visual impact from 30 quotations in green italics, many of these at the head of sections, and contrasting with the black roman text. In a sense these are, 'rather than data ... treated as illustrations and flourishes' (McGee with Brock, 2001: 34). But even decorations have their effects. Anyone skimming the WDR will have their eyes caught by these remarks. They might remind them that poverty and the bad life are not just words, but the experience of real people. The prominent quotations point towards policies; but their effect may be more through affecting policy-makers personally, as people.

Not all the voices got through. One big concern of many poor people was the police. Here the message in *Voices of the Poor* (pp. 162–6) is strong, stressing police brutality, harassment, extortion, corruption and unresponsiveness. Yet the WDR, strong though it is on legal systems and reforms, has little to say on the police.[26]

Perhaps the most conspicuous early effects of *Voices of the Poor* have been on policy-makers. Among international leaders who have quoted them, James Wolfensohn stands out, as with the words at the head of this chapter. He has repeatedly referred to *Voices*, and himself repeatedly amplified some of them. In a sense, he has enabled poor people to ventriloquize through him. Moreover, his many repetitions must have internalized them for himself[27] and impressed and influenced others. Big changes in development orientations and practice can be levered and catalysed by simple ideas. This one was that poor people's voices matter and those in power should listen to them. Coming from the President of the World Bank it carries weight and supports the big shift in development towards enabling poor people to express their realities and influence policy and practice.

That said, in the longer term, and in a wider perspective, the troubling question remains whether or to what extent *Voices of the Poor* has served as camouflage or cosmetic. Some might argue that it has been a disservice to poor people to allow the World Bank to present itself as a caring and listening bank. They might ask: has the wolf been helped to pose as a sheep? *Voices of the Poor*, they might say, can be seen as a diversionary tactic, a distraction from the main and major issue of whether the international financial institutions should continue to exist in their present form. A tough litmus test here is whether *Voices of the Poor* affects the middle management of those institutions.

To conclude on a positive note, there has been much useful learning about methodology (see, for example, Narayan et al., 2000b, Chapter 1 and Appendix 3). The methodology guide is available as a source of ideas for others. There was a healthy debate as to whether the Consultations had led at times to over-simple generalizations. Renewed discussion of the complementarities and tensions between qualitative and quantitative poverty appraisals has resulted.[28] The critical reflections of this chapter and elsewhere in this book have been provoked. Participatory methodology was spread to new countries and to researchers to whom it was new. The ethical issues of taking poor people's time and raising their expectations have once again surfaced.

Participatory appraisals and policy influence are increasingly localized – at national or subnational level – or concentrated on categories of marginalized and deprived people such as pastoralists, slum dwellers, street children, widows, sex workers and landless labourers. For these, there is much to be learnt from the Consultations concerning methodology, analysis, representation and influence.

Practical lessons for optimizing: trade-offs, balances, and win–wins

Of the practical lessons from the Consultations, some are old, some somewhat new.

- **Assess whether to engage**. When decisions are taken to engage in research there is usually some assessment of costs, benefits and risks, but less often of opportunity costs. Yet engaging in one research project can mean forgoing other opportunities to learn, influence and make a difference.

- **Self-critically reflect**. Perhaps the most important lesson is to be aware of one's power in the selection, organization and naming of knowledge. It helps throughout any research project to keep a self-critical and reflective diary and to revisit this. Much otherwise is forgotten. Much may also be distorted later through unconscious manipulation of memory, especially if there have been differences of opinion. The very act of writing a diary also helps reflection, optimizing trade-offs and identifying and adhering to principles which should be non-negotiable.

- **Optimize trade-offs**. Recognize and make conscious decisions about trade-offs both in the use of scarce resources, and in optimizing between incommensurable values. Some of the more obvious are:
  1. Scale and representativeness versus quality – the larger the scale the greater the level of representativeness, but the more difficulty in assuring quality.
  2. Scale versus timeliness for training, fieldwork and analysis – the larger the scale, the more time and resources needed for training, fieldwork supervision, and analysis.
  3. Scale versus resources for follow-up – for a given level of resources, larger scale diminishes scope for follow-up with communities, and for policy-related workshops.
  4. Standardization and analysability versus open-endedness and difficulty of analysis.
  5. Care and comprehensiveness of analysis versus timeliness in influencing policy.
  6. The qualifications and nuances of academic standards versus simplified messages for policy influence.

- **Adopt, invent and use win–win methods in analysis.** Seek to minimize or avoid trade-offs by looking for win–win solutions where there are gains all round:
  1. Develop and use a wide repertoire of diagrams, choosing those that fit the nature of the material rather than fitting the material to the diagram. Consult de Bono (e.g. 1981), Buzan (1974) and Waddington (1977) to extend the range and inspire inventiveness.
  2. Make verbal presentations. Do not limit communication and learning to the written word. Talk about experiences. In talking we say things that we do not write, and often express them more vividly.
  3. Write on cards. Note striking points while others talk. On other cards write impressions and understandings, what stands out, what seems to matter.

4. Sort cards into emergent categories on the ground. Express, cluster, and analyse disparate information in self-organizing ways, which also allow and encourage committed participants to contribute from their experience and critical reflection.
5. Revisit primary sources. Maintain self-critical doubt about conclusions, and return repeatedly to the originals to check, correct and reinspire.

Conclusion: reflexivity, power and pluralism

The biggest lessons I draw from reflection on these processes concern power and knowledge. This is not the common truism that knowledge is power. It is that power forms and frames knowledge and that interpersonal power distorts what is learnt and expressed. There is no full escape from this. Each one of us has to take responsibility for our part in the methodological, epistemological and ethical struggle to achieve representations of realities which optimize a multitude of trade-offs. There is no simple answer. But this chapter underpins three affirmations that help in finding good ways forward.

The first is honest reflexivity. Self-knowledge is so difficult that 'honest reflexivity' is almost an oxymoron. But difficulty is no reason for not trying. Degrees of understanding can be gained through introspection, and through observing, remembering and interrogating the interactions which fashion knowledge.

Unfortunately, the public expression of reflexivity, and hence our collective learning, is inhibited in three ways. The first constraint is personal, the fear of exposing oneself. Here social anthropologists have often set a fine example,[29] describing their own experiences, emotions and limitations, and reflecting on how they learn and mislearn. Those in other disciplines may feel more constrained by anxiety that self-criticism will ricochet.

The second constraint is collective loyalty to colleagues and friends. This can apply in any collaborative venture. In a research project in South Asia in the early 1970s I never sought to publish a paper 'Up the Garden Path'. It would have shown that in interpreting part of the results of a questionnaire survey the investigators themselves appeared to be the most powerful independent variable. As a finding it was important but disturbing. It would have upset colleagues and might have cast doubt on other analysis which we were publishing together. Rightly or wrongly, faced with this conflict of incommensurable values, I opted for personal relationships over professional responsibility. One can ask how many shortcomings of collaborative research are underreported and underrecognized for similar reasons.

The third constraint is space and time. In their late stages books and articles often lack space. They are considered too long. Editors and publishers demand shortening. Where are the cuts to be made? Methodological issues were the last part of the book or article to be written. They are also the easiest to cut.[30] Writing has taken longer than expected. The author or authors have run out of time and energy to argue. Further critical reflection is out of the question:

the team has dispersed; new research projects are in hand, or new jobs started, and neither time nor funds are available for further writing. So methodology and critical reflection are abbreviated, relegated to appendices or footnotes, or excised altogether.

The practical conclusion is to give space, time and rewards for critical reflection, and for collaborators to accept methodological criticism in a spirit of trying to help all of us to do better.

The second affirmation concerns how power distorts. Much power resides in patronage and the ability to bestow prestige. Anyone with these forms of power is disabled by how they attract and reward others. In this context, the World Bank is especially disadvantaged.[31] Perhaps the most painful but for me most important reflection concerns ego. Others will know whether they are also vulnerable and vain. It is flattering to be invited to Washington. It is great to be able to return to one's institution and write a trip report, as I did, saying that our workshop had been addressed by James Wolfensohn at a time when he was exceptionally busy, including in it the quotation at the head of this chapter, glowing with pleasure that he had said that our work was immensely important to him, and that he needed us to help him. 'Where have you been?' 'Oh, I see you were at the Bank'. And then casually dropping names. The very way in which we talk of 'the Bank', as I have in this chapter, reflects its extreme status and power: there is only one 'the Bank' and everyone knows which it is.[32]

A recurrent theme in this essay and in this book as a whole is another form of power: the power to frame the realities of others. As described, one of my activities was searching for material and quotations concerning themes or aspects I had identified as important. The example I have given of the body as a neglected aspect of deprivation illustrates the point. I was alert for and sought relevant evidence. The evidence was there to be found. But the process and its dangers, in my hands or in those of others, must be recognized. Nor are these dangers at all limited to qualitative data. Indeed, the authority commanded by statistics can make quantitative data even more vulnerable at times.

When these two manifestations of power combine, hazards are compounded. The incentives and temptations to please power are strong. The selection and manipulation of data are later invisible. Consultants and researchers show what is wanted and are not shown up. They then get further contracts. Prestige and promotion follow, in whatever organization. So it is that a synergy of patronage and the power to produce knowledge fabricates fantasies. As a post-modern Lord Acton might have said, 'Power tends to deceive and absolute power deceives absolutely'.

The third affirmation is pluralism. When there is consensus among those with power, warning lights should flash. Disharmonies are of the essence in much great music: progressions of discord resolve in transient harmonies, not once but again and again. So disagreement and debate are of the essence in learning to do better in development. In this context, those with power have learning disabilities to recognize and overcome. The experience of

Consultations with the Poor has proved a source of practical lessons. Not least it has shown what participatory approaches can achieve and how important it is to reflect on power, process and representation. In the methodology, epistemology and ethics of participation and policy influence there are no simple solutions. Rather there is a struggle without end to optimize trade-offs between conflicting values and to find good ways forward. For development to be better, many voices will always need to be raised, both of the poor and of self-critical development professionals.

Notes

1. For stimulating comments presenting a range of views, suggestions and corrections based on drafts of this chapter I am grateful to Karen Brock, John Gaventa, Rosemary McGee, Deepa Narayan, Andrew Norton, Raj Patel, Patti Petesch, Jules Pretty and Meera K. Shah. The experience with Consultations with the Poor, and the time to write this chapter, were supported variously by DFID, SDC and Sida. Responsibility for opinions, errors and omissions is mine alone, and should not be attributed to any organization or other person.
2. Consultations with the Poor describes the 23-country study that was one element of the Voices of the Poor project; its findings were published as Narayan et al., 2000b. The other element consisted of reviews of existing PPAs and other participatory research on poverty; findings were published as Narayan et al., 2000a and Brock, 1999. The whole initiative was originally called Consultations with the Poor but adopted the title Voices of the Poor in late 1999.
3. The study was led and managed by Team Leader Deepa Narayan, Lead Social Development Specialist in the World Bank's Poverty Group. Consultants Patti Petesch and Meera Shah played a major part in coordination and logistics, and methodological guidance and training, respectively. All three were involved in analysis and synthesis. The Process Guide can be accessed at <www.worldbank.org/poverty/voices/reports. htm>. For a description of the study process, experiences in the field and critical reflection, see Narayan et al., 2000b, Chapter 1. Chapters 2–11 of that book present findings. Chapter 12 is 'A Call to Action: The Challenge to Change'. Appendix 1 acknowledges many others who contributed to the study; Appendix 2 lists countries, sites and criteria for selection; and Appendix 3 provides an overview of study themes and methods.
4. A total of 272 sites is listed in Appendix 2 of *Voices of the Poor: Crying Out for Change* (Narayan et al., 2000b) and the figure is used for consistency in this chapter. However, the actual number of site reports available was somewhat fewer: for example, the 40 sites in Vietnam were summarized in four regional reports. If these regional reports are taken as site reports, the total is only 236. There were no national synthesis reports for Egypt or Sri Lanka. The Sri Lanka work followed a slightly different methodology but was broadly comparable.
5. In a three-volume series entitled *Voices of the Poor*, the first was a parallel book based on comparative analysis of participatory poverty assessments

(Narayan et al., 2000a). *Voices of the Poor: Crying Out for Change* (Narayan et al., 2000b) was the second and *From Many Lands* (Narayan and Petesch, 2002) the third, with contributions from countries that took part in the Consultations.

6. While contributions were made by other members of the Participation Group at IDS, those most concerned were John Gaventa, who provided overall management, Karen Brock and myself.

7. The World Bank is staffed by people who combine to an extraordinary degree intelligence, ability, drive and a range of views regarding 'development'. 'The World Bank' as I use the term refers to characteristics which are repeatedly manifest, and which damp down or override individual idiosyncratic deviance.

8. The word 'shortcut' was introduced by an editor into an earlier version before it reached Michael Cernea, in whose book it then appeared as 'Shortcut Methods of Gathering Information for Rural Development Projects' (Cernea, 1985).

9. For example, a trainer in Nepal who refused a contract because it required PRA training to be conducted in three days. She insisted that a longer period with fieldwork was essential. She was told that if she would not do it, someone else would be found who would. Someone else was found, and she lost the contract.

10. PRA, originally Participatory Rural Appraisal, now sometimes Participation, Reflection and Action, is an approach, methods and behaviours for enabling local people to undertake their own appraisal, analysis and action. For a fuller description see Chambers, 1997, Chapter 6 and <www.participatorymethods.org>.

11. See Yates and Okello, 2002.

12. See Adan et al., 2002.

13. *The Process Guide* (World Bank, 1999) was prepared by Meera Kaul Shah under the overall supervision of Deepa Narayan, Team Leader, and is available at <http://siteresources.worldbank.org/INTPOVERTY/Resources/335642–1124115102975/1555199–1124138742310/method.pdf> [accessed 28 July 2013].

14. Sceptical readers are invited to read and judge for themselves. The National Reports are on the same website.

15. Sources included card sorting for emergent categories in PPAs in South Africa (Attwood and May, 1998: 125), in Shinyanga, Tanzania (Gaventa and Attwood, 1998), and in the Empowerment Zones Programme in the USA (Gaventa et al., 1998).

16. For another example of SOSOTEC, see Kumar, 1996. This is a report compiled on the basis of 25 persons' experiences shared over 36 hours. More detailed descriptions of SOSOTEC can be found in Chambers, 2002 and at <www.participatorymethods.org/>. However, Meera Shah (pers. comm. 23 Jan 2001) found the 'ahhas!' or surprising and significant insights from the presentations of the team leaders more useful as starting points than the outputs of the SOSOTEC process.

17. Kath Pasteur, Anna Robinson-Pant, Damien Thuriaux, Kimberly Vilar and myself, with support from Karen Brock.

18. This is part of a listing by Meera Shah (pers. comm., 23 January 2001) which had overlaps with what those at IDS also found striking. From her analysis of gender relations she added: the reported trend of decreasing violence against women; the perception of many women that they felt an improvement in their status; and male frustration and anxiety.

19. Sequences vary. Andrew Norton has described (pers. comm.) a process which starts with the material. '1. Writer picks up an issue from the material. 2. Writer creatively formulates the issue in a way that makes it come alive personally in the light of own experience, concepts, values. 3. Use of the new concept enables writer to uncover other elements of the material which she would not otherwise have seen.'

20. It is bemusing to note that a regular dodecahedron has regular pentagons as its faces.

21. Other numerical analysis was conducted in parallel by a team at the University of Maryland. Details are not known or their objectives, methodology or findings. Examples of conventional tables with large numbers generated through participatory methods include a survey of utilization of services in some 130 villages in Nepal (ActionAid Nepal, 1992) and research into how poor people coped with the drought of 1992 in 20 districts in Malawi, Zambia and Zimbabwe (Eldridge, 1998). Both these generated tables are similar to those from questionnaire surveys. See also Mukherjee, 1995; Chambers 1997: 122–5; and Rademacher and Patel, 2002.

22. In spite of this, the usage crept into the World Development Report 2000/01. On page 146 it says 'In every part of the world participants in the *Voices of the Poor* study mentioned child labor as an undesirable coping strategy'. This is misleading as the study was not in every part of the world and child labour was not mentioned in every report.

23. An extraordinary example was the widespread belief that post-harvest losses at village level were of the order of 30 per cent. This had a life of its own in the 1970s and 1980s, persisting long after scrupulous field research had shown it to be a wild exaggeration.

24. I am grateful to Caroline Moser (2001) for the term and concept 'apt illustration', which comes from the work of social anthropologists Max Gluckman and Clyde Mitchell some 50 years ago.

25. The old usage of income poverty described simply as 'poverty' slips back, however, in later sections of the WDR, e.g. in Box 1.8 'Tracking poverty in India during the 1990s'.

26. In the 17 paragraphs of the WDR on poor people and the rule of law, only two sentences mention the police (on p. 103).

27. Catechists and teachers know how repetition embeds words and ideas, and any politicians who are critically reflective will recognize how this forms and distorts their beliefs.

28. Personal communication, Ravi Kanbur, who said that without *Voices of the Poor* and its impact on the World Bank, the March 2001 Cornell Conference on Qualitative and Quantitative Poverty Appraisal: Complementarities, Tensions and the Way Forward would probably not have taken place.

29. I am grateful to Paul Spencer for many anecdotes about his own work. See also Evans-Pritchard's classic account in *The Nuer*, pp. 9–15, Barbara

Harrell-Bond's description of her own behaviour in *Imposing Aid*, e.g. pp. 116–17; and McGee (2002). Another remarkable illustration is Elenore Smith Bowen's *Return to Laughter* (Bowen, 1956) based on the experience of her fieldwork, but written as a novel where 'the truth I have tried to tell concerns the sea change in one's self that comes from immersion in another and alien world'.

30. For example, when the edited chapters (Farmer, 1977) from a research project on agrarian change in rice-growing areas in India and Sri Lanka had to be shortened, it was precisely the one on methodology that was cut in length.

31. See for example Chambers, 1997: 97–100

32. Apologies to the African Development Bank, the Asian Development Bank, the InterAmerican Development Bank, and other banks. The statement here is about a fact of usage not of institutional reality.

CHAPTER 3

Ignorance, error and myth in South Asian irrigation: critical reflections on experience

As a researcher in South Asia in the early 1970s I was allowed to be seduced by the (then) neglected topic of water management and small-scale irrigation, which opened the door to a whole orchard of low-hanging fruit, much of it to be plucked simply by wandering around. This led later to time working on canal and other irrigation with the Ford Foundation in Delhi. There I was bemused by the close agreement of the World Bank and the Indian government, dishonest research, and absurdly impractical policies, until I began to understand the relationships and interests at play. My earlier naivety justified a consultant saying, 'You have to understand, this is India' – an India I did not want to recognize. With hindsight, I regret my reticence and timidity: whistleblowers are needed.

Keywords: blind spots, critical reflection, interlocking interests, research opportunism, wilful error, whistle blowing

The experience

In recounting experiences of three and four decades ago, I recognize the fallibility of memory and the ease with which we reconstruct events and experiences to flatter ourselves, show others in a less favourable light, and fit the occasion and audience. What follows is vulnerable to such distortions. Reader, be warned!

The theme that weaves through these reflections is how with irrigation we learn and mislearn, our blind spots, errors and myths, how these are generated and sustained professionally, personally and institutionally, and the implications of these for practice. It draws on experiences in South Asia as a field researcher over two years in the early 1970s and then with the Ford Foundation in Delhi for three and a half years in the early 1980s.

With hindsight I see that I have been fortunate in the freedom and opportunities I have had during my professional life. This has allowed me to change organizations, activities and topics. I owe this to a tolerant and adaptable family, a base in the IDS, Sussex, which allowed me to work with other organizations and in other countries, and a series of mentors, managers, funders and colleagues who gave me space and freedom to be a nomad who

http://dx.doi.org/10.3362/9781780448220.003

succumbed to the lure and excitement of emerging topics, abandoned plans, and did things I had not planned to do. Without that freedom I would never have become involved in water management and irrigation.

The first experience in 1973–74 was with research on the green revolution – or lack of it – with rice in South-east Sri Lanka and South India. I was a member of a team recruited by Benny Farmer, then Director of the Centre of South Asian Studies at Cambridge (Farmer, 1977). I was to work mainly on agricultural extension and research. A major questionnaire survey was managed by colleagues. I soon ran into difficulties with agricultural extension. Field staff were unwilling to share the reality of their lives and work, in part because they falsified their diaries. Agricultural extension was anyway well worked over as a subject, fashionable but less important than many believed, and less than thrilling. In contrast, we quickly found that water mattered much more to farmers than agricultural advice, and water supply and distribution were surprisingly full of intriguing gaps in knowledge. To my good fortune Benny Farmer, Barbara Harriss, John Harriss, Hiran Dias, Nanjamma Chinnappa and others on the project allowed me, even encouraged me, to try to find out and understand more about what we loosely called water management, in this case village-level minor irrigation and individual farmer lift irrigation. I was free to do almost anything and spent months wandering around, observing and asking questions in villages, and benefiting from brainstorming with my generous colleagues and from their insights and ideas. They helped me to learn how the water-related practices in the Indian villages we were studying varied to an extraordinary degree.

This led later in 1981–84 to appointment as a Programme Officer/Project Specialist with the Ford Foundation in Delhi, including responsibilities for irrigation (this now including canal irrigation) shared with others (Norman Collins and Roberto Lenton, who in turn managed our rural development group, and David Seckler and Deep Joshi). This gave exceptional access to Indian policy-makers, the World Bank and other aid agencies, research organizations and researchers. I was invited to workshops and conferences, and had time and opportunities to wander around and to write. As a grant-making programme officer I was hopeless, and probably the lowest performer the Ford Foundation had ever had. But as the last Project Specialist (the designation was soon abolished) I had scope to spend time on other things. I was also the social scientist in the three-person team that produced the report that was the basis for setting up IIMI (the International Irrigation Management Institute). Later, based on those years in India, I wrote *Managing Canal Irrigation: Practical Analysis from South Asia* (1988, Oxford and IBH Delhi, and Cambridge University Press), in which learning, ignorance, blind spots, and error and myth were major themes. I had been simply astonished by what I had come to learn about these and professional and personal motivations and mindsets. What follows here draws on and supplements some sections of that book with more personal experiences, some of which it did not seem fitting to write about at the time.

Learning, ignorance and blind spots

Let me take learning first, because it is through learning that ignorance and blind spots come to light.

Of course learning comes from many sources and experiences. But on reflection I am struck by how much of mine came from ground-truthing. This was through wandering around with more curiosity than agenda, observing and being inquisitive, asking questions and listening, but not doing these in depth with anything like the sustained intensity of a social anthropologist, rather looking for surprises and making comparisons, albeit superficial ones.

In the 1970s, rice green revolution research owed much to the contributions of others – the 'investigators', who learnt a lot on the side while carrying out the questionnaire survey, and John Harriss, who had many deeper insights. He and I shared a fascination with comparisons between the 12 Indian villages where research was carried out. Each of them had a different system for acquiring, distributing and allocating minor irrigation water, and each differed in its groundwater conditions. We came to realize that had I, or we, studied only one village, we would have supposed that its system was the norm, when in fact it was unique. The norm was the uniqueness of diversity. (From my days as a history student, I remembered how the stereotype of the Norman manor in England was for long based on one example, following which a succession of scholars announced that they had found an interesting 'exception', leading at last to the insight that 'exceptions' were the norm).

Two experiences, almost epiphanies, stand out. The first was a wonderful day in the early 1970s with Madduma Bandara in a tank command near Kataragama in Sri Lanka. We paddled through the flooded paddy fields and followed the water to see where it went. We found to our surprise that water in the drains was reused, in fact sometimes more than once. Farmers built brushwood weirs to raise the water level in the drains so that they could supply their fields. So one could understand why, when there was continuous flow and generous water in the head reaches, irrigation systems planned to be long and thin became in practice short and fat. And water-use efficiency had, we realized then, to take account of this unplanned reuse.

The second was in the early 1980s, wandering around in Uttar Pradesh on different occasions with Tushaar Shah, Niranjan Pant and Deep Joshi, finding out about lift irrigation. We stumbled on water markets: some farmers sold pumped water to their neighbours. This raised a host of questions about power supplies, costs, competition, reliability and pricing. As an economist Tushaar was enthralled and never looked back. He opened up the subject and soon became and has remained the leading authority on water markets in India (see for example Shah, 1993).

After we had tumbled to how widespread water markets were, we went casually and unannounced to an accessible and much visited World Bank tubewell designed to supply water to perhaps 50 to 100 farmers. We found that unlike the many other World Bank tubewells that had been installed in UP, this one shared the exceptionally reliable round-the-clock electricity supply of Lucknow. Moreover, the subsidized water supply had undercut the local water market with unknown effects on farmers with wells who sold water. Being unofficial wanderers we learnt more bad news about unreliability of water supply, defective construction and so on, all likely to be missed by brief official visitors who would then leave with falsely favourable impressions. So this World Bank tubewell was a specimen in the family of much-visited 'islands of salvation'. Unperceived by Bank staff, when these tubewells were installed all over the Gangetic basin they were duplicating, displacing and undermining existing water markets and livelihoods. One can only speculate whether, had these negative externalities been factored into the World Bank's project appraisal, there could or would have been any such World Bank programme at all; and without the programme, how much unaccounted, out-of-sight damage would have been averted, and how many millions of dollars saved.

That these findings about drainage water reuse and water markets were new to us must appear quite extraordinary today. But they point to a lesson about ignorance, and not knowing what one does not know. They underline the enduring importance of unstructured visits, curiosity and observation. Had we been informed by consultants' evaluations or officially orchestrated tours or conventional categories or questionnaire surveys based on the professional knowledge of the time, we would almost certainly have been denied these discoveries.

Some ignorance, we came to learn, clustered as blind spots. In the early 1980s, two of these came to stand out. The first and more important was main system management of canal irrigation systems (Wade and Chambers, 1980). Repeatedly evidence pointed to this as a priority for improving performance: farmers raised it again and again; and oversupply of water in head reaches and little and unreliable supply or none at all in lower reaches was an endemic pathology. On the larger canal systems in India this affected the productivity of water and land on millions of hectares and raised big issues of equity. Yet main system management was not a priority: in the professional training of irrigation engineers and their textbooks it was no more than an insignificant aside; engineers' skills, mindsets and personal financial interests through corruption all attracted them to construction, not management. Lenders and donors also liked construction because it was easier to disburse large sums quickly on infrastructure, which was also more physical and visible than management. So main system management was still in the early 1980s largely a blind spot, an area to explore and try to bring further into the light. Almost inevitably it had to be a wave of the future.

A second blind spot was irrigation at night. On major and medium systems, especially at tail-ends, and with electricity-powered pumpsets with irregular power supplies, this was when much irrigation took place. Wandering around was less convenient at night, and I did little of it: research at night means lack of sleep, discomfort including cold, difficulty seeing things, some danger such as slipping and falling, snakes, and risks of violence when illicit activities are encountered. So for years I kept a box labelled 'irrigation at night' and filled it with quotes, anecdotes and snippets from here and there until I could write an article and book chapter (Chambers, 1986; 1988). I calculated that on major and medium irrigation in India about 40 per cent of irrigation water was either applied or wasted during the hours of darkness. Irrigation at night appeared then to be an important subject and one about which little was systematically known. But I am not aware of any effect that either the article or the book chapter may have had. To my knowledge there has been hardly any follow-up. I mention this because not all ignorance is wilful or of disreputable provenance: some is sustained by simple inconvenience.

The origins and resilience of error

With so much freedom, both in the earlier South India and Sri Lanka field research and in the later years with the Ford Foundation, there was time and opportunity for flexible opportunism and for reflection, combined with privileged access, allowing critical participant observation of policy and practice. Again and again this revealed not just ignorance but stubbornly buttressed and defended fortresses of error. This had several dimensions.

Some of the resilience of error was sustained and reinforced by repetition and uncritical publication. Here are two examples: the first is embedded false statistics, the second is the much frequented and cited 'islands of salvation'.

A case of false statistics concerned the area waterlogged under canal irrigation in India. This was repeatedly quoted as 6 million ha.[1] In the early 1980s the then Secretary for Irrigation told me that when a parliamentarian asked what this figure was based on, he traced it to a Five Year Plan, which in turn cited a publication of the Administrative Staff College of India. He sent for a copy of that to be hand-carried by air from Hyderabad to Delhi, only to find that it in turn cited the National Agricultural Commission of 1976, at which point he gave up. Having more time, I indulged in statistical archaeology and found that the National Agricultural Commission was citing the 1972 Irrigation Commission. There the figure included 1.85 million ha in West Bengal where it must have been mainly from flooding as the net canal irrigated area in 1997–98 was only 0.96 million ha, only half the area reported waterlogged. The lesson was to doubt simple, memorable statistics that many embed and believe through repetition, and to dig down into their archaeology.

The second was frequently visited 'islands of salvation', which were then repeatedly cited and quoted backwards and forwards as personal experience to give and reinforce misleading impressions of feasibility and actual or potential scale. Three stood out: Sukhomajri (Seckler and Joshi, 1982) in Haryana where my Ford Foundation colleagues facilitated a remarkable degree of equity through allocating tradeable water rights to the landless – it received so much attention that for a time the Ford Foundation rented a place to stay in nearby Chandigarh; the Gram Gourav Pratishthan (GGP), an NGO in Maharashtra with a charismatic initiator and patron, Solanki – the GGP allocated water on a per capita basis (enough for half an acre of irrigation per family member); and most markedly and misleadingly of all, Mohini[2] in Gujarat where a high-profile cooperative system was rewarded with and sustained by a specially reliable water supply and other privileged access. Mohini generated a widely publicized, and almost totally false, impression that there were many water cooperatives in Gujarat and that these provided a model replicable elsewhere.[3] I confess that I was seduced by Sukhomajri and the GGP and urged their adoption elsewhere. Both were much visited: when I went to Sukhomajri I was in trouble because I took the best guide, denying him to a large party of important officials whom I then bumped into doing their circuit with a lower status guide; and the Sukhomajri school had a small forest of Eucalyptus planted by distinguished visitors whose memorial plaques were a who's who of the agricultural establishment of India and of international organizations. The Sukhomajri and GGP approaches never spread.[4] Both were far too idealistic, sharing water democratically in ways that could not be reproduced. But for a time, in writing after writing, in workshop after workshop, in conference after conference, in keynote address after keynote address, they were cited as feasible ways forward to a fairer and better future. For myself, I was part of all this, and far too naïve in my optimism. Such is the power of repetition, reinforcement and wishful thinking.

Warabandi: power, ignorance and error

One advantage of unstructured visits in various states in India was the start of an understanding of water distribution systems' effects on major canal irrigation. The most famous and widely lauded distribution system was *warabandi*, designed into the large systems of North-west India. David Seckler went into this in detail. We came to learn that *warabandi* was in part a myth, as its practice diverged from its elegant theory. But that only adds to the force of what follows. In the theory of *warabandi*, continuous and constant flows through outlets are shared between farmers day and night for fixed periods during each week. The time allocated to each farmer is proportional to landholding size. *Warabandi* depends on four conditions: a steady supply assured by fixed outlet apertures well below an assured canal full supply level, combined with rotation between distributaries and minors for periods of whole weeks; channels to supply water to individual farmers' fields; low rainfall; and identified land tenure for the allocation of timings and turns. These conditions existed in North-west India but probably nowhere else. The first in particular was critically missing outside the North-west as most systems elsewhere had gated outlets and relatively low canal water levels. Where this was the case, constant flows through outlets could not realistically be assured and the system would be unmanageable and a complete nonsense.

As a system, though, *warabandi* was regarded as exemplary. A booklet by a distinguished engineer, S.P. Malhotra (1982), describing its seductively elegant mathematics was accessible and had attracted attention. So *warabandi* was on the agenda of a two-day workshop for the highest level irrigation engineers in the country to discuss policy for the next Five Year Plan. As a courtesy I was invited. To my amazement, horror and disbelief (and self-doubt – surely they *must* know more than me, and know what they are talking about, and who am I, an ignorant unspecialized social scientist from another country, to say anything?) they believed or spoke as though they believed that *warabandi* could be spread throughout India. I felt they must surely know something that I did not. I may have tried to speak up, but if I did it had no effect. I do not recollect any other voice being raised. A collective delusionary consensus prevailed. A target was set of 8 million ha to be achieved in the Seventh Five-Year Plan period. The outcome was major investment in metal *warabandi* boards giving fantasy timings erected to rust and decay all over India as monuments to top-down ignorance and folly.

The above paragraph is what I wrote in the first draft of this essay. Gil Levine made a wise comment on the draft: 'I do think that the knowledge and understanding that many in both the donor/lender and recipient sides have is better than would appear, but the institutional imperatives are such that they effectively mask much of this understanding.'

This gave me pause for thought and prompts another explanation: that some or many of those present in the meeting did indeed know that *warabandi* would not work outside the North-west. But they may also have known that World Bank loans (and patronage – see below) were at stake, that big budgets were projected, that department status and prestige were at stake, even perhaps that the 8 million hectares had already been mooted and agreed. To raise questions would have been to rock the boat and perhaps even to prejudice one's career and prospects.

Whatever the truth, and it is unknowable, the cognitive and behavioural lock-in of some combination of ignorance, power, prudence, deference, institutional politics and/or tacit connivance over *warabandi* was far from limited to the senior engineers of the government. It was also reinforced by the World Bank and its interest in making loans, and its commitment to timed turns in irrigation.

The visit of Daniel Benor, the charismatic and highly influential consultant to the World Bank, came to be, for me, a spectacular eye-opener. Benor was highly respected as a major authority and international figure for his propagation round the world of the disastrous routinized Training and Visit (T&V) system of agricultural extension. As that was gradually being exposed and abandoned as a costly failure, he moved on to irrigation, where the rigid, mechanistic and timed *warabandi* system had much in common with T&V. Roberto Lenton and I were invited to join him on a field visit to Andhra Pradesh. I think only I could go. I was flattered and went, hoping to learn from him. One day stands out vividly. Benor would only speak with farmers, not officials. Time and time again he questioned a farmer and soon the farmer would be saying, yes, what they needed was timed turns between farmers on their irrigation systems. I was impressed and in awe of his empathy and ability to relate to farmers, and to their unanimity in coming to realize that they wanted timed turns. Only later did I learn from Robert Wade what must have been happening. He had discovered during fieldwork in Andhra Pradesh how for occasions like this farmers would be coached by officials for hours beforehand on what they were to say, and that above all they must agree with what the important visitor wanted to hear. These farmers, carefully chosen and coached, knew what was expected of them, and agreed as soon as they could with what they could tell Benor wanted. These interviews were followed in the evening by a meeting with about 100 farmers. Benor said how impressed he was that they all wanted to rotate water supplies below the outlet. Then one farmer stood up at the back and objected. The problem was not rotation, he said, it was of getting water in the first place. The tail-ends did not get water. 'Sit down', he was told. Courageous man, he held his ground. 'Sit down', he was told again.

The farmer was right. Many leads were telling us that management of canal main systems was a massive blind spot and priority. The overriding need was more equitable, predictable and reliable distribution of water above the outlet. But Benor and the Bank did not seem to want to know about main system management (though this began to change while I was with the Ford Foundation). They had their solution and some were not interested in farmers' problems. I had to conclude too, that, perhaps even more than the senior engineers, Benor simply did not know the necessary physical requirements for timed rotations to be workable. We were concluding that the major problem and opportunity on canal irrigation systems was not distribution in the chak below the outlet but management of the main system to assure a reliable water supply, especially to the tail-ends.

Designing research to 'succeed'

My self-doubt and disbelief were also deep when it came to related research conducted for the World Bank by a consultancy firm, WAPCOS. I had difficulty believing what I found.

The background is that both the World Bank and senior officials wanted construction programmes with big budgets. Their motivations varied. No doubt there was an element of engineering professionalism preferring and valuing construction over system management. More important, perhaps, in the World Bank there were incentives of prestige and promotion in making bigger loans. For their part, senior government officials were all in favour of budgets of construction programmes with their high expenditures and opportunities for patronage and corruption.[5]

But there was less and less scope for construction of new systems: the better sites had been taken, and major construction, apart from the notorious and contentious Narmada project, was going out of favour. A growing impediment within the Bank itself was the strong movement, courageously led by the redoubtable gladiator Michael Cernea, for adequate safeguards and compensation for those displaced by dams. So some other way of continuing investment in construction had to be found. A solution was sought in building structures below the outlet. This fitted nicely with the related World Bank interest in rotating water supplies to farmers. The proposal, then, was to build structures so that water supplies could be rotated between new subchaks of 8 ha each. But research was needed to justify this. So WAPCOS, a large consulting firm that did much work for government and the Bank, was commissioned to establish what benefits there might be from such a system comparing it with current practice. They did this on two systems in Madhya Pradesh.

Their report of 1980 was not easily accessible. Its conclusions were summarized in the public domain (Chadha, 1980; 1981) as reduction in the time taken to irrigate the entire chak – 5–14 days compared with 20–45 days for normal chaks without subchaks, and yields 70–137 per cent higher than under normal outlets. The field studies '... demonstrated dramatically the effect of delivering water through government-constructed channels up to smaller chaks (of 8 ha in this case). ... Our recommendations, supported by field studies carried out as part of consultancy services, are for 8 ha subchaks ... It is a matter of happiness that Government of India also accepted these findings and have issued new guidelines on the subject' (Chadha, 1980: 388).

I do not recollect how I eventually got hold of a copy of the full report. As soon as I had it I spent two whole days analysing the data. It took so long because I could not believe what I was finding. I went over the data again and again. Each time my findings held up.

The evidence in the report in no way justified its conclusions, Chadha's recommendations or the government policy. None of the alleged benefits were supported: neither acceptance by farmers, nor reduced time taken to irrigate the whole chak, nor yield, nor uniformity of yield could be attributed to rotation of water between the subchaks. The data had been generated, manipulated and interpreted in ways which were at best careless, naïve or unprofessional but at worst and most probably knowingly dishonest and designed to mislead.[6]

The research was designed, implemented and analysed to ensure that the intervention was a 'success'. The full detail is tedious. But for the record some of the main flaws and biases were:

- There were 3 intervention chaks and 11 controls. Of the 3 intervention chaks, 2 were eliminated, 1 because it received very little water and 1 because of a severe gall midge attack. None of the 11 controls was eliminated.[7]

- The single surviving intervention chak, Koliary, on which all the conclusions were then based had these special conditions (among others):
  - location near the administrative headquarters in Raipur;
  - location at the head of a minor, itself at the head of a distributary at the head of the system, so with exceptionally privileged access to water;
  - farmers were assured a reliable water supply if they would adopt high-yielding practices, including chemical fertilizer inputs;
  - bank loans, fertilizer and HYV seeds were arranged and assured.

These were enough to demolish any credibility in the report. I was incredulous and nonplussed that any self-respecting firm could be so unprofessional or that the Bank or the government could accept 'results' which were so patently and transparently bogus.

What the data from the 11 control chaks did show, reinforced by Koliary, together with a broader survey analysed by Roberto Lenton (1983), was quite different: yield varied with position on the main system. The conclusion justified by the data was not benefits from rotation below the chak (treatment of Koliary was so exceptional that if rotation between subchaks had had adverse effects these would probably have been masked by other special conditions), but the priority of improving management and water distribution on the main system. That was not what WAPCOS had been funded to find. That was not the tune the piper was paid to play.

I wrote up my (I thought devastating) analysis and sent it to the Bank and to WAPCOS. It was greeted with the proverbial deafening silence. But I persisted and eventually a discussion was arranged. Only WAPCOS was there. After a superficial exchange, it was suggested that I go into more detail with a single staff member. So we went into another room. It was impossible to engage seriously. He kept sliding off the point. Then after a bit he said to me, 'You have to understand, this is India'.

As for the Bank it never did engage and for whatever reasons (prudence, social, political or other priorities; see below) I gave up, but in a rather academic way put it all in *Managing Canal Irrigation*, published some five years later. There was no comeback. I doubt whether any of those concerned ever read it. They would by then anyway have moved on to other things.

This tale has three footnotes. First, by extraordinary coincidence, one Saturday afternoon I was stranded in Raipur for a few hours between trains. I decided to try to find the officer in charge of Command Area Development, and tracked him down in his home. He was welcoming and delighted to talk. He went out of his way to tell me how he had supervised the research and given special treatment to the Koliary chak, ensuring its water supply, and making sure that the bank loans, the HYV seeds and the fertilizer were all available to all the farmers. He was proud that he had made the research a success.

The second footnote is that ten years earlier in the Philippines Tom Wickham and others had conducted professionally rigorous research on a similar intervention of subdivision and rotation between subchaks. They found that yield differences between treatment and controls were not significant (Wickham et al., 1974; Lazaro and Wickham, 1976; Wickham and Valera, 1978). Nowhere could I find any reference to this highly relevant research with its unwelcome finding. I concluded later: 'The investigation seems to have set out from the start not to learn but to "succeed"; not, that is, to conduct a scientific investigation of causality, but to show that the chosen intervention made things better' (Chambers, 1988: 59).

I could have been bolder and left out 'seems to have'. Others might have been more outspoken and said that it was grossly unprofessional by all concerned, a case of wilfully generating false findings to justify a costly and dysfunctional project that was likely to be against Indian interests. The 'matter of happiness' about the findings was however shared by WAPCOS, Government of India officials and the World Bank. WAPCOS had done their duty and gratified the bank and the government, no doubt assuring future contracts. The bank was justified in making large loans, good for disbursement and for careers. And the government was able to continue construction with its patronage and ample scope for rents. Win–win. What a system!

The third footnote is whimsical. When angry I sublimate through verse. This experience provoked:

How to Succeed with Irrigation Action Research

(Delhi, early 1980s)

> Rural development's all the rage
> and irrigation's reached the stage
> when funds will flow if you can say
> action research is on the way.
> The title's new, the techniques old,
> the pickings rich for all the bold.
>
> Success eludes none but those fools
> who do not heed some simple rules.
> Reconnaissance you do not need.
> Prepare your programme with all speed.
> For what to test no need to care,
> choose any dogma that you hear.
>
> Field levelling and OFD,
> eight-hectare chaks, warabandi,
> lining the channels or rotation
> conjunctive use, participation –
> pick any action that you will;
> if fashionable, it fits the bill.
>
> To choose the site, criteria
> are simple, obvious and clear.
> The most important one by far's
> a tarmac road for motor cars.
> As well, it must be close to town
> for rapid transit up and down.
>
> Make sure the water flow is steady.
> Have your staff there always ready.

If water's short at system level
get it first and let the devil
take the hindmost at the tail.
For science, your interests must prevail.

Make sure the biggest farmers gain.
Their PR's needed to explain
to VIPs on their brief stops
the splendid impact on their crops.
(Small farmers should not be a worry
No one will meet them in a hurry.)

Recruit the bankers to your team
and organize a credit stream
Good fertilizer, HYVs
and pesticides are sure to please.
And if you want to get first prize,
why then it's best to subsidize.

So when it comes to harvest day
you'll be all right – thanks NPK!
Crop-cutters, here's the patch of field
where you will get the highest yield.
And none will know you are a liar
if you make it even higher.

If any area does badly,
cut it out, reject it gladly.
Say special factors made it fail –
a water shortage, pests or hail.
The only truth there is to tell
is found in places which do well.

So all is fine. You have succeeded.
The will to win was what was needed.
The yields are treble, water half,
you at the back, what makes you laugh? –
the farmers, they are satisfied.
It shows how very hard you tried.

Thus is achieved the vital task.
In praise and glory humbly bask.
Honoured for service and devotion –
who knows? – you may now get promotion.
If others fail to replicate
Poor honest fools, that is their fate.

Political economy and 'the system' of professional, social and personal relations

In Delhi it took me quite a long time to fathom how the system worked. On a personal and social level there was a self-sustaining nexus of professional, social and personal relations, with a political economy linked to careers and income. Let me explain.

For a long time I was bemused to understand how and why the World Bank and the Indian government always seemed to agree on irrigation policy and projects, and why they would virtually connive in what seemed wilful ignorance and myth as if they did not want to know the truth. Being as I was both close and yet outside, I could see that this seemed to apply to almost every aspect of irrigation policy. This was not just over *warabandi*, or the programme for infrastructure in the chak below the outlet. Another example came from two consultant engineers of impeccable integrity who did work for the Ford Foundation. They found falsification or a false calculation in the figures used to justify raising the level of the Sardar Sarovar dam. How could this happen? Who else knew about this? Who knew but did not want it to be known that they knew? How could people get away with such things?[8]

Gradually I came to see significant influences, and now five stand out:

1. The most obvious was the common interest in large loans. Having a big budget and being able to disburse it in a timely fashion was good for both World Bank and GOI staff. This was a major driver.

2. Officials gain in status and power by working on secondment to the World Bank or on a World Bank project. They would proudly give me their cards with World Bank printed on them. I overheard officials asserting their power to get things done by saying, 'The World Bank is coming'. On one possibly apocryphal occasion a Bank official and his opposite number were arguing and disagreeing in front of other Indian staff. In a tea interval the Indian said to the Bank person, 'For goodness sake. You are weakening. Don't!' He must have needed to be seen to be dominated and overruled by the Bank. Such tacit or explicit understandings may be widespread, but I have never seen them noted in the literature.

3. Much less obvious was the patronage of World Bank consultancy or employment. World Bank fees or salaries were much higher than those of the government so it could pay personally to get a good reputation and then employment with the bank. Also significant was the prospect of consultancy after retirement from government service. I only realized this when I was invited to a Bank retreat of its staff together with consultants who were commissioned for work on rural development. A significant proportion of those present had been at the top of the irrigation hierarchy during the last two or three years of their careers and on retirement had been hired by the Bank. One could understand that others at the senior policy level with similar hopes would be inclined to agree with whatever the Bank wanted.

4.   Then there were institutional interests affecting us all to some degree. Our organizations needed good working relations with others. In the Ford Foundation we had a lot of independence and support from whoever was the Representative, but all the same it did matter that we got on well with the government. There was always the lurking possibility of causing an upset and having to answer for it.

5.   Finally, there was a social dimension of dinner and cocktail parties, children at the same school, friendships and the Ford Foundation swimming pool. The prevalence and significance of dinner parties is easy to exaggerate – it is in my experience an overblown stereotype; but cocktail parties could be important for the wider mix of actors they brought together, the ease of meeting and talking across levels in hierarchies, and the opportunities for networking and informal communication. Schools were also important among expatriates. Many in the Bank, the Ford Foundation and bilateral and international agencies had children who went to the American school (as two of ours did – the third went to the English school); through the children, their friends and parties, relationships and friendships developed also between their parents. Then for us there was the Ford Foundation pool on Lodi Estate. The World Bank offices were next door and World Bank staff – some of them at least – had access to the pool. We and our families often met there in the early evening for a swim and chat. So out of this came a sense of community and a reluctance, on my part at least, to be too proactive in confronting myth and error. I, too, was part of the system.

So what? Reflections on realism and how to make a difference

These experiences point to how power, budgets, professional training and orientation, personal careers and incomes, and social, institutional and political interests and constraints can interweave and interlock with ignorance, not knowing what is not known, and not wanting to know, and telling power what it wants to hear. This matters because in irrigation, as in other fields, ignorance, error and myth can lead to massive misallocation of resources, as they did with irrigation in India in the early 1980s.

How in conditions like these does one find out and learn, uncover blind spots, and make a difference?

On finding out and discovering and uncovering blind spots, what I learnt was the value of wandering around, and we learnt much as a result about both canal and lift irrigation. Such wandering around is best unannounced and done without ceremony. Governments, aid agencies, NGOs and many academics are hopeless in the extent to which they fail to recognize and practise this. They allow their staff to be overloaded and tied down in offices, and trapped in capital cities by meetings, administrative procedures, visitors, workshops and much else, and so to be out of touch and out of date. Time and resources have to be ring-fenced for unstructured visits. This is as vital for good development practice as it is impeded by the current results-based culture, among aid agencies at least. As it is, such opportunities for learning are largely confined to consultants and junior researchers.

On influencing policy and practice the lesson was the lack of straight lines. There are tangled webs of intertwining interests, commitments, perceptions and misperceptions, tacit unspoken understandings, diplomatic silences and unseen processes. I was one of those arguing for priority to main system management, and writing about it. But I do not feel there was much direct success. In the Ford Foundation we could have indirect influence by negotiating and making grants for research, by writing, and by discussions with a wide range of actors, but these were at several stages removed from major decisions and actions. A minor wrinkle on this, to be noted with a wry smile, was that because we had ourselves some limited patronage through grants, our views were sometimes treated with unwonted respect and deference: people would tell me how valuable and insightful they had found my writing. On two occasions a consultant who worked for the Foundation gave keynote speeches to which I listened, nodding with appreciation for their sound sentiments until I realized that he was parroting verbatim whole chunks of my writing (was this plagiarism or flattery?), but this at least gave them a wider circulation and authority.

The scope for influence through negotiating grants seemed obvious but could be constrained. The best grantees were already overcommitted with projects. Grantees who had been overpersuaded could drag their feet. And in practice in those days grants would overrun. Or what happened would differ from what we had expected. The elastic between local priorities and those of the Ford Foundation could also be overextended. The Foundation had women's participation as a priority. Roberto Lenton and I visited the Mahi Kadana project in Gujarat with this high on our agenda. The engineers who greeted us had organized a day's visit around *their* agenda – rising water tables. We stared in dismay at seriously saline soils and wondered how they could conceivably be linked with women's empowerment. Somehow a project was put together, but I did not envy Lincoln Chen, the Representative, having to justify it in New York.

Probably the biggest opportunity for influence I had was as the social scientist on the three-person team set up to consider (this was a third attempt) an international organization in the CGIAR to be concerned with irrigation. The leader was Ernst Schulze, who had a physical and agricultural sciences background, and the other member, Philip Kirpich, was an engineer. It seemed to me vital that any such institute should have a strong social science orientation, and give some priority to main system management on large gravity irrigation schemes. The three of us got on well, but I sensed a danger of too strong a technical orientation. I remember the last days of drafting in Wageningen. I had gone into special training so that I would be fit and alert and able if necessary to outwork and outdraft the others on that final push. For whatever reasons, the report got a fair wind, and IIMI[9] was set up in Sri Lanka. Tom Wickham was the first Director-General, Roberto became the second and David Seckler the third. And they did indeed have a huge and formative influence through their position.

For realism, reflexivity is one key, being aware and critical of social, political and personal factors that distort perceptions, policies and practice. If perceptions are to be realistic, if policies are to be well-informed, and if practice is to be good, self-critical awareness is vital. I do not think we are at all good at this in development practice.

Finally, to bring realism and influence together to make a difference for the better, a key ingredient is honesty and courage. Here with hindsight I regret my reticence and timidity. My failures stand out. I did not confront power face-to-face. Had I been a different person, I would have been more aggressive. I would have rocked the boat. But then I was a staff member of the Ford Foundation, which had its own political position to protect, and what I found out and came to understand was not part of any formal terms of reference that I had. But I could and should have spoken up about *warabandi*. I could and should have confronted Benor. I could and should have persisted in exposing fraudulent research. It is very late – three decades too late – to say all this. I only hope that it will encourage others to be bolder so that policies and practice can be better grounded in realities and so that they better offset the professional, institutional and personal forces that so easily distort perceptions and generate and sustain misleading and damaging myths. We need not just to struggle to know reality. We need whistleblowers and we need them to blow more and a good deal louder than I did.

Acknowledgements

For useful comments and suggestions about earlier drafts of this paper I am grateful to Roberto Lenton and Gil Levine.

Notes

1. I came to wonder whether there was something particularly memorable, or even transferable, about the 6 million figure, as it was used also by environmentalists for some aspects of land degradation. More detail and references can be found in *Managing Canal Irrigation*, Chapter 1.
2. For more on Mohini, see *Managing Canal Irrigation*: 59–62.
3. Robert Repetto (1986: 33) wrote that, 'In Gujarat State in India, the irrigation agency sells water volumetrically in bulk to cooperatives, which distribute it and collect fees from their members'.
4. However, the Centre for Science and the Environment in New Delhi kept a watching brief on this project and published brief reports on what they found in 1994, 1998, 2002 and 2007, concluding that Sukhomajri became a prosperous village, with household incomes double the average in Haryana as a whole. It was able to sustain that prosperity over time, while at the same time adapting to profound institutional and environmental changes. Though not replicable, the changes in Sukhomajri were then deep, lasting and positive (pers. comm. Roberto Lenton).

5. I do not wish to imply that all officials were directly corrupt. However, Robert Wade's (1982) seminal article exposed the widespread and deeply rooted system. Construction generated huge rents (as much as 50 per cent of the budget). Irrigation officials bought their posts, priced according to their perceived potential pickings. At one time a donor could not understand a three-month standstill in an aid process, as I recollect, for rehabilitation of tanks in Tamil Nadu. The reason, I learnt, was that the engineers who could bid for the post of managing the project considered that the rents had been overestimated and the post overpriced.

6. For a fuller and slightly more qualified analysis, see my book *Managing Canal Irrigation* (1988: 54–9).

7. For a more nuanced and qualified analysis see *Managing Canal Irrigation*: 56. The main points do, however, stand.

8. Their finding was less surprising in the light of the subsequent Independent Review of the Saradar Sarovar dam in the Narmada valley led by Bradford Morse (Morse and Berger, 1992). They concluded that the Bank had seriously violated its own policies, that these violations had devastating human and environmental consequences, and that it was difficult to escape the conclusion that there had been gross delinquency (pp. 233–4 and *passim*). The Morse review led to setting up the Inspection Panel of the World Bank, which provided a mechanism to avoid repetitions of the Narmada case by giving voice to people who would be harmed by such violations (pers. comm., Roberto Lenton).

9. The International Irrigation Management Institute. Before this name was settled on there was, though, much debate about what to call it. This became quite a cliffhanger. Nothing seemed quite right:

> So we can't have Service, and Centre's out;
> we're feeling nervous, time's running out;
> let's call the brute an Institute,
> but that won't do – an institute's too formal too.
> Consortium? Consociation? Cadre? Cluster? Federation?
> Core? Or Corps? Or Core Corps? No – it's more like Archipelago.
> Headquarters, Focus, Node or Hub are too damned central, that's
>   the rub.
> Bureau's too office-bound, the field is where we find all truth
>   revealed,
> and Agency's a private eye or CIA, a public spy.
> The situation's really grim, I do not feel my mind's in trim.
> INTRIM!? Thanks, Freud. You're just in time to give the name and
>   one last rhyme,
> International Network for Training and Research in Irrigation
>   Management.

PART II

Exploring learning

CHAPTER 4

Learning about learning

This selective account of personal learning describes aspects and lessons that I hope will be of interest and use. The deepest learning has come from quite intense experiences such as: the thrill of ahhas!; the discovery that 'they can do it' (local people have far greater capabilities than most professionals give them credit for); and finding out much that is new and unexpected simply by wandering around, observing and being curious. Other keys to learning include, 'failing forwards', disempowering oneself to encourage critical feedback, doing the more adventurous thing, and play and fun. Seeing, feeling and acting out roles make for more powerful and deeper learning than most insights at a purely intellectual level. The guiding slogans are dare, risk and hand over so that you can learn from what others do. The chapter concludes with 21 tips (read at your own risk) to help and encourage other nomads on their learning journeys.

Keywords: adventure, ahhas!, 'ask them', critical reflection, curiosity, experiential learning, fun, modes of learning, play, 'they can do it'

In Chapter 1 I described the outline of my changing personal orientations and trajectory, notably how it took me long to recognize my managerial and top-down mindset and to offset that. Elsewhere I have described the extraordinary experience of being a participant in the evolution of Rapid Rural Appraisal and Participatory Rural Appraisal (Chambers, 2008b: Chapters 4 and 5). Here I shall draw on and analyse those and other experiences, adding other recent ones to identify how I think I have learnt and perhaps others learn and can learn. This leads to the final section: 'Twenty-one tips for nomads on learning journeys', which I hope other explorers or would-be explorers will find useful.

As I described in Chapter 1, I have been exceptionally lucky in the freedom and opportunities I have had to be around at the times and in the places where I have been. Few other people have had such good fortune. The conclusion could be, then, that the examples of learning that follow and the inferences I draw from them for learning about learning will be less relevant for others. My own view is that these points are generic, related to our human condition and that they can apply anywhere and in any context. The relevance and intensity of experience will vary. But I hope that teasing them out and describing them here will encourage and support others to see themselves as explorers and learners on a daily basis, enjoying the thrills of discovery in what otherwise might appear routine, repetitive and ordinary life.

http://dx.doi.org/10.3362/9781780448220.004

Ahhas! The thrill of discovering that 'they can do it'

Let me go straight to the excitement. This was the thrill of ahhas! – the eureka moments when scales fall from the eyes; or at least that's how they seem with hindsight. At the time mine seemed less dramatic than they do now. Indeed one of the great dangers I found was actually not noticing what was truly remarkable. Looking back, there were many ahha! occasions when ordinary rural people, literate or not, women or men, older or younger, poorer or less poor, showed they had a capacity for complex analysis through their mapping and diagramming that neither I nor others had suspected: a farmer in Tanzania who drew on cardboard a map of the agro-ecological zones of his village; farmers in Gujarat who kept and updated their own-hand drawn map of underground aquifers; four groups of villagers in South India who counted the population in their village and all came up with the same figure of 355; two women farmers in Kenya who drew and scored for importance the numerous nutrient flows on their farm.[1]

Two other examples were a sequence of discovery. The first was in a small hut in Ethiopia in 1988.[2] Two Ethiopian colleagues interviewed three farmers using a series of questions we had devised. These asked of a number of items which was more and which less. We would then draw a histogram bar chart. In this case it was for the amount of agricultural work by month. When my colleagues drew the chart on paper, I did not think the farmers would understand it, but we asked them all the same. They looked, checked and said: 'Yes, you have drawn what we said'. This led on to a second occasion, in West Bengal, when a group of scientists and I asked tribal men if they could do the same for men's agricultural work this time drawing on the ground. They amazed us by drawing a histogram, outlining it with rice powder. We asked women to do the same, which they did. But then they argued among themselves, and added a big block at the bottom of their diagram across all the months, saying that this was all their other work of cooking, cleaning, fetching water and the like.

A dramatic case was in 1989 when a group of us stayed four days in Kalmandargi, a village in Karnataka in India. This was the first occasion which we could describe as PRA. Jimmy Mascarenhas, then with the NGO MYRADA, arranged our stay in the village. We were trying to explore the limits of what villagers could do. We asked a few of them if they could make a model of their village. I was then away for two or three hours. When I came back they had dug up a grassy patch and used coloured rangoli powder to create a spectacular 3-D model of their village and its watershed. They were full of pride and enthusiasm. They had even put in the poles for the electricity which had recently come to their village. One of them said: 'I have always wanted to do something like this'. Later, I showed a photograph of their model to the staff of a high-powered regional remote sensing agency in Hyderabad. The Director asked: 'And how long did it take you to train the villagers to do that? One year? Two years?' It was embarrassing to have to tell him in front of his staff that they had done it on their own, straight off, with no training at all.

Another scales-from-the-eyes experience was in the second PRA in another village, Kistagiri in Andhra Pradesh. In fieldwork in Tamil Nadu 15 years earlier I had tried to map the wells in a village. I spent two days on it, and finally gave up. In 1989 in Kistagiri Sam Joseph asked the villagers to do the same thing. It took them about 25 minutes. At the end of that time they had drawn a map showing their wells, about 50 of them; and they had marked those which were good and those which were dry. They knew.

Or again, in May 1991 farmers in Nepal used seeds and sticks to show days and volumes of monthly rainfall.[3] In 'But how does it compare with the *real* data?' (*RRA Notes* 14) Gerry Gill compared their data for volume with 20 years of records from the nearby Lumle Agricultural Research Station. He found the farmers' data more relevant for agriculture. Moreover, they also included a five-yearly abnormal year with snowfall which the station did not record.

Experiences like these led us to the behavioural principle of assuming that 'they can do it' – that if we as facilitators have confidence in local people and encourage them, then women and men, poor and rich, able or not able to read and write, can present and analyse the complex realities of their lives and environment through mapping and diagramming, and do this to an extent that few if any of us 'professionals' had ever dreamt. Those who in context were 'lowers' to me and my colleagues did things we could not or did them much better than we could. This was startling, sobering and a bit humbling, but at the same time a source of amazement, delight and learning. We found that this goes for facilitation too. Peers were better at facilitating their peers than were we outsiders: certainly villagers could be better facilitators of other villagers than I could ever be. After the first shock and adjustments, we learnt how making space for 'lowers' to take over one's 'upper' roles could bring its own fulfilment.

Wandering around, observation and curiosity

In any busy life time is quickly crowded with activities; diaries get overfull; things which cannot be done at once are written in for later dates. It is a variant of the classical Alice-in-Wonderland syndrome of running as fast as you can to stay in the same place – in this case running as hard as you can to protect any spare or unplanned time. Like many others I suffer from but also enjoy this state of busyness.

The casualties in my life have been family, friends, even holidays. I have also lost the learning, ideas, reflections which can come with inactivity or doing something entirely different. But here let me consider another casualty: failing to learn from taking time to be somewhere, with whomsoever, and simply wandering around, noticing things and being curious.

When wandering around, there is a danger of day-dreaming, thinking about something else, or walking past without seeing something. Well, you do *see* it but you do not *notice* it. I do this more and more. In a PRA village stay in Karnataka where a major concern was watershed management I walked right past a wall and was yards away before I stopped myself and turned round to see what it was. Farmers had built their own anti-erosion work that was trapping silt to make a fertile field. This led to my noticing many more small works that were easy to overlook.

Then there is not taking time to explore. In an RRA training in Dessi in Ethiopia, we were applying some of the methods and approach of agro-ecosystem analysis developed by Gordon Conway and colleagues at the University of Chiang Mai (Conway, 1985). Part of this is the transect, the systematic or not so systematic observing walk through an area. Everything of interest appeared to be concentrated near the roadside – people, houses, cultivation. Above was dry grazing land. When we mentioned the transect to local government staff, they said there was no point going up there, there was nothing up there. It was clear it would take at least a couple of hours, walking over land that from below looked all the same. A waste of time. But anyway (perhaps I wanted some exercise) with some grumbling we went. Exploring 'nothing up there' turned up a significant discovery: half-hidden gully fields. These were micro-environments in erosion gullies built up over years by adding to barriers of big stones, each year trapping more silt. Protected from sun and wind by the gully walls, these were sheltered and exceptionally fertile fields. In semi-arid conditions where they 'would not grow' they had dense crops of chat, coffee and vegetables. If we had not used our time 'badly' by doing the transect, we would never have known.

One delight over four decades has been a habit of jogging before breakfast, wherever I am. On workshops and conferences and trips this takes you out of the hotel or guest house and into another world.[4] There are dangers of getting lost (twice – once in Dakar, once in Dhaka),[5] dog hazards (terrifying in Hyderabad, Bangkok and Kathmandu) and traffic (worst ever, despite the name, in Jogjakarta), and not even getting out of the hotel (in Tehran, stopped for wearing shorts), but these have been offset many times by unplanned experiences and pleasures of the unknown.[6] Every jog is an exploration.

Failing forwards

Small children learn at phenomenal rates, some, I have been informed, at the rate of a word an hour. They do this by failing at phenomenal rates. They fall when trying to toddle. They make endless mistakes when trying to speak. But they do not mind. As Dr Zeuss said, 'Adults are obsolete children'. Part of our obsolescence is that we try not to make mistakes. We do mind when we make them. We do not fail forwards, much. And so we learn slowly.

If children are anything to go by, there can be more to learn from failures than successes. If so, our biggest failure may be failing to learn from failure. Mistakes, errors, things which do not work are swept under the carpet, not reported, concealed; so are considered negative when they could be positive for learning. How often do we hear, 'Well, that didn't work did it, *good*! What can we learn?'? Not often.

Engineers Without Borders (Canada) has set a fine example with its annual Failure Report.[7] This 'allows us to share the lessons more broadly and create a culture that encourages creativity and calculated risk-taking'. At the annual conference in Canada to which some 500 people have been coming, the Report is presented and celebrated. And lessons are learnt.

Failing forwards also fits a turbulent world of accelerating change. Continuous learning and adjustment are in paradigmatic contrast with long drawn-out rigorous research. Each has its place but failing forwards belongs with adaptive pluralism and a world and contexts of complexity and emergence.

That the Chinese word for crisis also means opportunity is quoted often enough to be a cliché. But the truth it tells has for me again and again been evident. The most common has been having to improvise when something breaks, breaks down or is left behind. Electricity failures in South Asia forced improvisation when I could not present a slide show. Or I went to the Netherlands for a workshop and left much of my gear behind. Almost without exception, what happened was better than it would have been. Improvisation tends to be participatory, and I can recollect BRAC staff in Bangladesh mapping and diagramming on the ground when I had dropped and damaged the British Council projector and could not show them the slides I had prepared, an animated discussion in darkness by scientists in Dhaka for an hour when the lights went out, and the success of NGO staff in the Netherlands mapping, sharing and commenting on the layouts of their offices – none of which would have happened without the provocation of the disaster. Best of all is when the disaster jerks you out of a rut of routine into which you never fall back.

Disempowered for feedback

Being treated with respect is a learning disability that goes with age (until senile and treated like a child or infirm)[8] and power. I know I am vulnerable to this. Critical feedback is precious, something to be treasured, and sometimes the more painful it is, the more valuable it is. Here are two examples.

I was invited to Iran by the Ministry of Jihad.[9] We were about 25 people. I started as usual inviting everyone to write their name on a sticker so that we could know what to call one another. At some stage in the morning I sat on the floor in the middle, with the participants all on a higher level sitting round, and practised 'shut up!', the very difficult activity of deliberate silence. Usually after a little time people start talking among themselves. On this occasion one participant addressed me directly, and told me that at the start of the workshop I had done something culturally insensitive in asking everyone to write their first names on their stickers – which obediently they had done, but these were not the names they used.

In the mid-1990s three of us from IDS were involved in disseminating PRA and supporting IIED's efforts to seed and support networks. There was an international workshop of networks on networking in Nepal. We discussed our hopes for the workshop, and wanted to know what we should do to 'hand over the stick', sensing that we were too central and wishing ideologically to be egalitarian and to promote South–South relationships. My two colleagues, Heidi Attwood and Kamal Singh, went and asked the question. The memorable reply came back: 'Who are you to say that you have a stick to hand over?' We were not that central or important. My head had been too big.

In both cases the feedback went deep. The fact that I remember these two incidents speaks for itself. The lessons were to disempower oneself and to 'ask them'. Intentional silence (Kaner et al., 1996) is difficult to practise if you are facilitating or lecturing and in full flood with adrenalin and enthusiasm, feeling you are expected to fill space and time with speech. But silence empowers others. And non-verbals can help when seeking critical feedback – not standing, folding arms or crossing legs but sitting, sitting lower, sitting in a non-dominating position, even (I have been told) opening hands upwards. And best of all, and sometimes the most difficult, overcoming the idea of being indispensable, and simply not being there.

Learning, feeling, changing

I am struck by how much more we learn and internalize through seeing things through emotion rather than through analysis. To be sure, there are many conceptual, intellectual and factual things that are learnt by reading, analysis and reflection. But there have been occasions when whole mindsets have changed in a day. I have known wonderment when this has happened to others. In the first PRA in India, in Kalmandargi, a Soil and Water Conservation Officer began a day in a village lecturing to farmers. Then we did an extended transect and noticed farmers' own extensive soil and water conservation measures. He had never noticed these before; at the end of the day he said it had been one of the most remarkable days of his life, and never looked back.

But more than just seeing, these moments or occasions which are life- and behaviour-changing experiences typically involve strong feelings. This has been most marked with what at the time felt like negative experiences. I mentioned some in Chapter 1 – having my written English sharply criticized when I thought I knew perfectly well how to write; being told that I had a managerial mindset, always taking the side of the management, when I thought I was balanced and impartial; being turned down by an appointments board when with my big head I thought I deserved promotion. These all hurt. Precisely because of the mixture variously of shock, humiliation and pain, they were also all seminal in making me change.

A variant on this is 'See-Feel-Change' (Kotter and Cohen, 2002). Applied to organizational change, this is the idea of showing people something which is striking and evokes emotions that then provoke action and change. This is also the principle manifest in the effectiveness of triggering in community-led total sanitation (CLTS) (Kar, 2003, 2010; Kar and Bongartz, 2006; Kar and

Pasteur, 2005). Communities who defecate in the open, when facilitated to see the realities of what they are doing and how 'they are eating one another's shit', are so disgusted that they resolve to do something about it. This can take immediate effect, and can lead whole communities to making themselves Open Defecation Free (ODF) in weeks or months, after many years of teaching and instruction have had little or no effect. It is emotion, the emotion of disgust, that drives action and change.

Learning by acting

Some of the deepest and most enduring insights have come from role plays which speak truth to power. In an ActionAid workshop in Dhaka we did a power pot exercise where people stood close or far away from a pot according to their relative power. Those of us who stood closest to the pot were embarrassed at the visible manifestation of our position and acted the fool. This then became the subject of quite deep reflection. Or again, in a District in Uttar Pradesh, an NGO partner of ActionAid role played a visit from their ActionAid programme officer: the preparations and distortions which could be made explicit were both frank and funny. Yet for all this I am inhibited as a facilitator and still hesitate to invite role plays or acting. Intellectually I know this is wrong; emotionally it reflects my timidity, and perhaps a hangover of English inhibition.

That said, some of my most enduring learning has been through designed and structured role plays such as the Green Revolution game designed by Graham Chapman, Africulture by Janice Jiggins, and further developments by John Thompson.[10] These games are played in a room, usually in a full day including reflection and discussion. Players draw families with different resource endowments, and make decisions season by season, experiencing the uncertainties and choices facing peasant producers. In India Barbara Harriss-White and I paired off as a couple and were dismayed when we drew lots and found ourselves the richest family in the village. We had hoped to be poor and powerless and to understand better what that was like. But we had to accept our destiny and resolved to be generous and make sure that no one in our community suffered. We tried to make this known. It was only when the game was over that we learnt that two people had died of poverty. They were in our village, but even in the room they were physically at the edge, in a corner, right at the margin; and no one had told us. We had not noticed them, interacted with them or sought them out. We had been so busy with the management decisions to take, season by season, with all our land and wealth, that we had no time for anything else. Lessons like this you do not forget. You learn. The learning is embedded. But you do not know, cannot know, in advance what you will learn.

Role plays in workshops are also memorable. Alan Margolis gave a training to 25 of us who were involved in the early days of PRA. One of his exercises was to challenge us in small teams to take an hour and prepare a one-minute (strictly timed) cameo to get across a message. It was not easy to do, but we were under time pressure with the sure sanction of public exposure at the end of the hour. I do not remember any of the other presentations! But in ours we stood naked except for big nappies, fell down in turn at two-second intervals, with a bald loud statement at 55 seconds that, 'Every two seconds a baby dies from preventable causes'. You remember what you take part in.

Daring, play and fun

Fun is a human right. By that I mean that everyone should have the space and opportunity to play, laugh and enjoy. It is a sad fact of our world that there are so many millions for whom misery, suffering, abusive life experiences and infirmities rule this out. The human right is to conditions and space for play and fun.

The downside of not wanting to make mistakes or fail is playing safe, sticking in ruts, avoiding unfamiliar or uncontrollable situations, not taking risks. But good new things often come precisely from facing the unfamiliar and uncontrollable, and by taking risks. All those long Latin words – creativity, adaptation, spontaneity, inventiveness, improvisation, innovation, originality – that express so much that we say we value also feed into and are fed by the simple monosyllable dismissible as frivolous – fun. With all these comes learning.

Take play, for instance. Young animals and young humans learn about their bodies, their environment, the boundaries of what works and what does not, what they can do and what they cannot, through trial and error, much of it in forms of play. They are explorers par excellence. And as they mature they play less and explore less. When and if humans go to the great majority of secondary schools in the world, the top-down discipline of learning by rote or something close to it and reproducing what the teacher says or the book asserts deadens play and playfulness in the adolescent. So much institutional education drills out of us much of the capacity to learn outside the confining walls of convention.

A possibly apocryphal story is told of Kenneth Robinson. He was asked to convene a committee to consider creativity in secondary education. So he sought out some of the most creative people he knew. It turned out that about half of them had flunked or opted out of secondary school or university.

I have a problem here. My script as a boy was to get full marks and bask in parental and teacher approval. It has taken me many years to begin to realize how disabling this can be. In facilitating workshops, for instance, I again and again crawl into the security of 'something I have done before'. Each repetition that is not challenged or disastrous deepens the rut and makes it harder to break out.

Yet many of the best things have happened when I have dared or been forced to take risks, to try something threatening and new, lost control or handed over. I only realized my sense of identity as an explorer (Figure 0.1), which inspired the title for this book, because I handed over to a student to facilitate the end of a workshop. The lessons for learning are simple:

dare, risk, hand over.

Twenty-one tips for nomads on learning journeys

Writing tips like this may suggest I have things well sorted in my life. This is far from so. But enough has happened now to give clues and cases which point towards some tips. So here are ideas of what we can do. I hope they are sounder in their advice than I have been diligent in their practice. Please do not sue if following any of these leads you to disaster. 'The author accepts no responsibility ....'

1. *Disempower yourself*
   Examine your power, institutionally and interpersonally. Is it a learning disability? Does it inhibit and distort your learning? Do people tell you what they think you want to hear? Do you lack critical feedback? How much critical feedback have you had from anyone in the past week? Do you need to disempower yourself so that you can learn from others better?

2. *Reflect critically on your mindset*
   Reflect on how your life experience, disciplinary training, concepts, vocabulary and personal interests structure your view of the world. What are your favourite words? What do they tell you about yourself? Is what you find good? Does it matter? Is there anything to work on?

3. *Keep a reflective diary*
   If this is on your desktop or laptop and you want to keep it to yourself, hide it with an improbable label in an improbable place, but not so improbable that you forget it.

4. *Be alert for ahhas!*
   Keep awake and alert for the unusual. Remember that ahhas! are not all big and life-changing. They can be small things, but a source of pleasure and learning, and nice to share with others.

5. *Do something new*
   Try every day to do something new: explore a new place, follow a new route, eat a new food, read a new article or story, see a new video, play a new piece of music, meet a new person, remember a new joke, play a new game, entertain a new idea. At the end of each day ask yourself what new experience you have had. What have you explored or discovered? (I often forget to do this.)

6. *Suspect anything you often repeat*
   This may seem silly but in my case it is not. If you repeat something in public, in a speech or lecture or workshop, and are not contradicted, you are embedding it in your belief system. Moreover, when faced with an audience, you are liable to mould what you say – recounting an anecdote for instance – to fit the occasion and to sound and go down better. After a few repetitions the initial qualifications ('it seems likely that...' or 'very probably') slide into simple assertions which you (well, I) find I believe.

7. *Turn things upside down, inside out, back to front*
    This is the easiest route to originality. Take hold of the other end of the stick. See things from others' point of view. Stand on your head. Revel in reversals. Challenge convention from below, beyond, above, inside, outside.

8. *Work on your listening*
    Not listening must be one of the most widespread human failings, particularly among those who are energetic, fit, enthusiastic and committed. They 'love the sound of their own voice'. When with others how much do you talk, and how much do you listen? How many times during the day have you interrupted someone in the middle of their talking? Particularly anyone junior to you. What marks out of ten would you give yourself for listening to others during the day?

9. *If you end up where you planned to be, doing exactly what you planned, worry*
    It may be all right. You may be able to take legitimate satisfaction in ticking boxes. But does it mean that you have missed out on something? Did you have your head down so that you did not notice something new, or did not seize an opportunity?

10. *Ask who you 'other' and how they see you*
    When you talk, who are 'they'? Who do you 'other'?
        Who do you refer to as 'these people' or 'those people'? People of other ideologies, political parties, professions or disciplines, ethnic groups, genders, classes, education, tastes, habits, physiques, interests, clubs? What does this tell you about yourself? Does it matter? We all 'other' some people, even when this doesn't fit the flattering image of the humane, pluralist, tolerant, mutually respectful person part of us might like us to be. On the other side of the coin, how far can you go in seeing yourself as others see you, others who 'other' you? Might even partial success in confronting these questions bring rewards in understanding and relationships?

11. *Negotiate, analyse and maximize your room for manoeuvre*
    We all feel ourselves constrained but we all have some room for manoeuvre, room to make space for doing things differently, for doing new things, for exploring. Work on a strategy for widening that space and exploiting it

12. *Plan time for unplanned experiences*
    Many do not have this luxury. For the past few years I have tried to make it a rule on any travel to factor in one or two days at the end with no programme. Lamentably this is liable to be eaten into by feeling that I should catch up with emails. But several times it has led to good things I could not have known would happen.

13. *Co-conspire and collaborate with others on parallel learning journeys*
    You are unlikely to be on your own. Heretics, minorities, explorers, adventurers almost always have someone like-minded near them and can enjoy the rewards of solidarity when they discover one another.

14. *Do different things, and do things differently*
    Diversify your activities and experiences. Unless it is excessively expensive, dangerous, time-consuming, harmful for others, or bad in some other respect, when in doubt do the more adventurous thing.

15. *Treasure incidents, stories and jokes*
    Notice funny things that happen. Reflect that often the worse things are, the deeper a disaster, the better tale it will make to recount to family, colleagues and friends. Remember jokes (not something I am any good at).

16. *Transgress disciplinary boundaries*
    Trespass with confidence. Remember that your perspective and the ('naïve') questions you ask are likely to differ from those of others, and that those strongly specialized within disciplines often have a narrow view.

17. *Wander around*
    Wander around physically in any environment. Within (and on occasion beyond) the bounds of courtesy, be curious and inquisitive. Go where others do not go, or others like yourself do not go. Follow up on leads. When someone says they would like to show you something, accept.

18. *Look for gaps and connections*
    Look for gaps in knowledge or experience, and for neglected or unusual connections. Seek out and explore ungrazed pasture.

19. *Recognize and offset cognitive biases*
    Some biases are in mindsets. Some are embedded in and reinforced by preferred and habitual language and activities. Yet others are spatial; these may be the easiest to recognize and offset, as with those of rural development tourism.[11]

20. *Play around and enjoy*
    Don't take all this too seriously, and certainly not yourself. Take all this advice, which I do not that much take myself with a pinch or several pinches of salt. Anything that you try, make it into fun. Why not? Anything stopping you? Enjoy!

21. *Make your own list of 21*
    Don't be limited by these 20 points above. Disagree with them. Add to them. Draw up your own 21.

Notes

1. Reproduced in *Whose Reality Counts?* (Chambers, 1997: 139).
2. This was an example of co-innovating and learning through hands-on training, one of several ahha! discoveries during a field training exercise in Rapid Rural Appraisal led by Gordon Conway for the Ethiopian Red Cross (Ethiopian Red Cross, 1988). For photographs of this and other personal eureka moments, see 'Reflections and directions: A personal note', written for the 50th issue of Participatory Learning and Action (PLA, 2004).
3. For a photograph, see PLA 2004: 24.
4. One day I may put together a collection of accounts of these early morning jogs which have been a source of so much surprise and pleasure. But such place-dropping would be an ego trip and I doubt of interest to anyone else.
5. If you take to jogging in unfamiliar cities, take care to remember the name of the hotel.
6. This has included the serendipity of meeting other joggers. David Hulme I have encountered once in Dhaka and once in Rio de Janeiro, such is the similarity of our circuits, it would seem.
7. <http://legacy.ewb.ca/en/whoweare/accountable/failure.html> [accessed 25 August 2013].
8. For most of us this is not a sudden but a gradual transition. I treasure the indicators of the progression that I have noticed as I get older: being described as sprightly; being offered her seat by a young woman; being offered a wheelchair when standing in a queue; being described as 'institutional memory'; being addressed as 'we', a pronoun reserved for children, the very sick and the advanced elderly – 'how are we feeling this morning?', and (not yet in my case, but I have heard it) 'are we having a senior moment?'. Then there is forgetting that you have put some of this in another footnote already.
9. Jihad in this context was a metaphor for a campaign for rural development.
10. For Graham Chapman's Green Revolution Game and Africulture, see <www.future-agricultures.org/index.php?option=com_content&view=article&id=582:green-revolution-game-simulating-the-reality-of-small-scale-farmers-&Itemid=992> [accessed 19 November 2013].
11. For the biases of rural development tourism – spatial (urban, tarmac, roadside, airport), person (elite, better off, male, healthy, users of services, adopters of practices), project, seasonal (dry season), professional (focus on things of professional interest), security (visiting places that are safe) and so on, see the index of *Revolutions in Development Inquiry* (Chambers, 2008b).

CHAPTER 5

Participatory workshops: teaching, learning and large groups

Participatory workshops for teaching and learning have not been planned but have happened and evolved with a life of their own. In the course of this, approaches and methods have been borrowed, adopted, improvised and invented. Messing up, borrowing and trying new things over the past decade has generated tips and ideas for activities to prepare and conduct such workshops. Twenty-one of the best of these are described. They include preparations, sequences of analysis, finding out what sticks in people's minds, how what is right can be wrong, handing over the stick, teasers, fishbowl, intentional silence, a politically incorrect energizer, review and reflection, and talk–listen. The challenge of welcoming, mixing and managing large groups, for instance students from many countries who arrive for a course, has its own enjoyable repertoire.

Keywords: facilitating large groups, group dynamics, participatory workshops, trying new things, workshop practicalities

Explanatory prologue

Incompetence and ignorance can be wonderful triggers for participation – or at least that is how I have experienced them. It began in 1962 in the Kenya Institute of Administration with three six-month courses for Kenya administrators who were taking over from the colonial administration. As I confessed in Chapter 1 I did not know enough about anything to be able to lecture. So quite apart from imperatives of relevance and usefulness, I had no option but to devise participatory exercises. Fortunately this fitted well with the urgent demands of the time: experiential learning of how to do things was what the Kenyans wanted and needed and what we, the faculty, sought to provide. Repeatedly we found that it was better to facilitate than to teach. And the tradition of Harvard case studies, sharing experience, analysis and ideas, and moderating discussion rather than lecturing continued throughout my time later with the East African Staff College. Then when my passport said I was a 'university lecturer' I was spared actually having to be one: I never once had to give a lecture during my three years at Glasgow University. And later at IDS the five-week study seminars of the 1970s and 1980s for officials and others from developing countries relied heavily on case studies.

http://dx.doi.org/10.3362/9781780448220.005

It was, though, only in the later 1980s with RRA familiarizations and training, and the 1990s with PRA familiarization and training in IDS, Reading, LSE, Oxford, East Anglia, the London School of Hygiene and Tropical Medicine and elsewhere, that it all began to come together as an emerging and gradually cohering methodology. This led to a short book, *Participatory Workshops: A Sourcebook of 21 Sets of Ideas and Activities* (Chambers, 2002), completed twelve years ago in 2001. Since then throughout the 2000s to the present time of writing in 2013 I have had the opportunities, challenges and fun of trying to evolve and diversify these workshops. Earlier ideas and activities can be found in the *Participatory Workshops* book (henceforth referred to as PW). The sections most likely to be useful for teachers and trainers are probably:

- 21 ways to form groups;
- 21 arrangements for seating;
- 21 ideas and options for analysis and feedback;
- 21 ways to help each other learn;
- 21 tips on how to avoid lecturing;
- 21 tips for dealing with dominators and helping the silent speak (if they want to);
- 21 ways to not answer a question.

However, the most appreciated 21s, I have been told, are none of the above but:

- 21 tips for surviving participatory workshops;
- 21 horrors in participatory workshops; and most of all
- 21 mistakes I make in workshops.

On mistakes confessed, I have been told it is a relief to know that you are not alone in this: we all mess up, it is all right, it is not shameful, you are joining the club.

This chapter does not repeat the twenty-one 21s in PW. It adds to them from recent innovations, experiences, borrowings and learnings. 'Recent' refers to the past twelve years. There are once again compulsively twenty-one of them, I can't help it, for reasons explained elsewhere (PW: xv–xvi). They differ from the earlier 21s in that methodologically they are on the whole somewhat more generic: that is to say, their use can be versatile, not only for the contexts and applications mentioned but also for others. Finally, the third section of this chapter, 'Twenty-one ways of welcoming and mixing very large groups', describes methods devised, evolved and adapted for welcome workshops in IDS and the University of Sussex for groups of over one hundred students from many countries who do not know one another. I hope this menu will help teachers, trainers and facilitators, and tempt and encourage them to try out some of these ideas, to broaden their applications, to adapt and improve them, to launch out and explore for themselves in other ways and to share what they do with the rest of us.

Twenty-one tips and activities from ten years of messing up, borrowing and learning

1. Preparations

I have had to learn again and again to invest more time and trouble in preparations for workshops. I never seem to get this right. This is much more than just asking the 'Twenty-one questions when preparing for participatory workshops and learning' (PW: 4–6). Here are some basics which are easy to omit, skimp or get wrong:

Find and look over the venue. So often the rooms proposed are too small, too hot, too cold, too noisy (traffic, fans, air conditioners, heavy chairs that grind on the floor when moved), with thin walls (noise disturbs neighbours), with fixed furniture, wall surfaces which masking tape pulls away, leaving a legacy of pock marks, or on which a fussy management prohibits its use, or with no walls on which anything can be stuck. It is also easy to forget to check that the room will open an hour or more before the workshop starts and will remain open after it ends.

Ensure adequate gear. We all have our predilections. Take your own small reserve set of flip-chart pens, masking tape (which so often disappears) and pins. Request flip charts and flip chart stands, pinboards. See also 18 below regarding new (and old) gear.

Communicate with the participants in advance. It helps to establish contact, to tell whoever may come that they are welcome, and what if anything they need to do to prepare. Unless there are special reasons for restrictions, throw the workshop open to all comers, and refuse to allow a registration fee. Give an outline of purpose and approach without tying yourself to a rigid programme. Make people feel welcome and not in any way threatened by the workshop.

Prepare handouts, charts and lists of websites and other sources. If the workshop is any good a number of people are likely to want to follow up. A single sheet handout with a list of websites is good to take away.

Ensure coffee/tea/biscuits/lunch. Breaks and intervals are often the most useful times for participants, contrary to what we would fondly like to believe about our fantastic sessions. Make sure they are well set up, and don't rush them.

2. Documenting and sharing

For a good learning process documenting and later sharing can be a key component. In a participatory workshop where there are many activities and a good deal of movement, taking notes is neither easy nor even a good idea. A solution is to have one or more people who take notes for everyone else and share these later. They can be recruited beforehand, or volunteers. In either case, for subsequent distribution of notes have a laptop on which those who want to receive them type in their emails (this avoids misreading handwriting and emails bouncing back, and makes subsequent distribution straightforward). Use your judgement about whether you need to look over the notes before they go out: often I have found them very good, but once or twice they have needed considerable editing to make them more accurate and fuller in their coverage.

3. Who are we and meeting

Give some thought to the diversity and interests of those who are coming, both who they are and whom they may want to meet. There are many ways of facilitating introductions and meeting (see PW: 17–24 and other tips below). My biggest recent lesson is, when groups are formed around something they have in common, to be sensitive to how much time to allow for the spontaneous conversations and exchanges that spring up. They may need little time. Or they may constructively run on for ten minutes or more.

4. Finding out the experience and resources in the group

I am ashamed that there was not more of this in *Participatory Workshops* (see PW: 19). It was limited to asking participants what they hoped to contribute. I have since found that proactively seeking out potential contributors often pays off handsomely. This can be done in various ways. One is asking participants to stand between polar extremes such as lots of experience of a subject or activity and none. Another is to cluster around topics which they know about. In meetings with individuals or small groups, arrangements can then be made for them to facilitate or share their experience.

5. Hand over the stick

Many of the best things happen when others take over. I have found it helps to ask participants to take over, for instance taking and writing up feedback, while I can sit back and relax and regroup for the next activity. Some of the very best things – like the personal identity example (Preface) – have come from 'students'. A recent example was a whole hour – the graveyard hour after lunch moreover, which Effie Makepeace facilitated in a way that I could not have – engaging participants in standing in certain postures and then changing these, and leading on from this into theatre. Others have more guts and daring than I have, and it pays off handsomely.

6. Mixed pairs for sharing and learning

Where there is a contrast of experience, views, professions or other characteristics in a group, where some have something to share, ask participants to separate out or stand in polarized lines. Invite them to pair them off and ask, share and discuss. One example is old students and new students. The new students decide what they want to ask and the old students what advice they would like to give. They then pair off, or do this as small groups.

7. Sorting slips

This is an example of an effective and versatile form of judgement and analysis which enables people to come to their own conclusions. The underlying principle or hypothesis is that people can explore many topics through shared knowledge and analysis rather than being told or taught them. One application can illustrate. This is 'We Learn By...'.

Process: Tear up small slips of paper. Form groups. Ask groups to write on one slip each words such as reading, seeing, teaching, experiencing, doing, writing, repeating, talking and discussing, thinking, hearing.

Ask them to complete: 'We Learn By' by sorting the slips in a column graded with those they judge to be most effective at the top and least at the bottom. Walk around, compare and discuss, or string on masking tape and hang up next to one another for comparison.

Outcome: Learning by doing and experiencing usually come top, and hearing and reading at or near the bottom. This can then lead into a discussion of how students spend least of their time on the activities they learn most and best from, and most of their time on those from which they feel they learn least. This in turn can lead into discussion of how to do more doing and experiencing, and how to make better use of the time spent hearing and reading.

This outcome needs to be qualified by recognizing that we all have different learning styles. I have learnt to respect the fact that some from other cultures really like and prefer lectures to the more interactive learning which I favour. What we expect and are comfortable with from 'teaching' may or may not be for the best; and our ways of learning can change. Those who have taken part in the 'We Learn By' exercise may also be a biased group, self-selected people who like participatory modes of learning, which is part of the reason why they have come to the workshop, or the workshop has been made available to them. All the same, I have been struck by the high degree of consensus that has come from this exercise.

8. Sequences of analysis

Sequences of participatory analysis can be strong. One example is 'Personal and Professional Status' in which sorting slips provides the basis for analysis of implicit social and professional values.

Pre-prepare slips of paper with different professions and people on them for medicine and health, for agriculture, and for university departments. For medicine, for instance, it can be (in random order) GPs, sick women, consultants, hospital nurses, village midwives, keyhole and transplant surgeons, sick men, general surgeons, community health workers, trained midwives, traditional medical practitioners. Groups sort these in a column on the ground with higher status at the top and lower status at the bottom (status being what is, not what ought to be), first for medicine and health. When this is done, all walk around and compare. There is usually a high degree of consensus. Repeat this with slips for agricultural professionals and people in agriculture – agricultural extension agents, poor female farmers, wealthy female farmers, genetic engineers, participatory researchers, agricultural economists, laboratory researchers, research station field researchers, wealthy male farmers, poor male farmers, plant breeders; and then for university departments. The columns are laid out next to each other so that high and low status can be compared across them visually.

Ask what polar characteristics in practice contrast between high status and low status. Groups write these on slips (A4 paper will tear into three 21 × 10.5 cm strips), which they stick on pinboards, making columns of similar characteristics for ease of visual analysis. The outcomes are striking: high status – low status goes with men–women, specialist–generalist, dealing with things (or people as things)–dealing with people, high income–low income, working in highly controlled–uncontrollable environments, and much else, setting a rich agenda for reflection and discussion.

Three keys to this exercise are: visible, tangible and movable categories; analysis by participants; and discussion based on what can be seen and comes from their analysis. This method should have wide applicability wherever there are common knowledge, values and polar contrasts.

9. Repeating slogans

When I ask participants at the end of a day's workshop what their main take-aways are, they want to get away, and may find sound bites a way to keep it short and catch the train or bus. All the same, I have been struck by how often it is short slogans that I have repeated, and to an extent that they have used. These often express attitudes and behaviours. Some of the most common and potent come from PRA and are widely familiar:

- Ask them (the idea of asking others, often your team or your juniors, for their ideas and advice);
- They can do it (the idea of assuming that others, most of all lowers, can do something until shown otherwise);
- Sit down, listen and learn (the idea of coming off any pedestal and behaving as a learner);
- Use your own best judgement at all times (the idea of taking responsibility for your actions); and my favourite,

- Shut up! (oh! that more people would do this and listen and converse instead of lecturing, preaching and indulging in monologues. I could start with myself).

10. What sticks in people's minds

Once, a year later, I met a group of young people with whom I had spent a day before they left the UK for placements abroad. I asked them what they could remember from that day. The silence was ghastly. Then someone said, 'we played on the ground'; and someone else said, 'you held a map upside down'. And that was it. The playing on the ground was practical for participatory mapping and matrix scoring, two methods I thought they might find useful (and some did). This was learning by doing. The upside-down map was to show that how you see things depends on who you are and where you are: for the person holding the map and looking down, it is not upside down but the right way up. This was learning by being startled and shocked into seeing something differently. I am struck (learning by writing) that it is only on writing this that I realize that to the list of 'We learn By' (tip 7 above) should be added, 'learning by seeing things upside down, inside out, the other way round'. Doing that is fun and effective as a form of exploration.

There are though many ways of learning and many ways of exploring. Nothing here can aspire to anything like covering them all.

11. Telling stories, best against yourself

There is a widespread belief, popularized by Stephen Denning in *The Springboard* (2000), that stories can be powerful agents for changing mindsets and behaviours. I have no reason to doubt this. To a degree it is borne out by my experiences. When asked what they can remember from earlier workshops, it is often the personal experiences, especially stories against myself, that people retrieve from their memories. This led me to wondering whether I should go through life making more mistakes so that I can make the lessons memorable by recounting them to others. Anyway here is one:

White-water canoeing. I have only done this twice. The second time we came to turbulent rapids with water boiling around boulders that we did not know were there. There was no escape. There is no time for you to ask what it says in the manual. You just have to focus ferociously and fight to survive. I thought there was no way I could get through – life had been good while it lasted. But the amazing thing was that I did get through. And as I was coming out into the calm water below, I said to myself, 'Bloody hell! You've done it!' And that was when I tipped over.

The morals of the story are obvious: in white water, manuals are of little use; and the moment we relax, thinking we have arrived and made it, is when we tip over.

12. Wrong can be right

One of the hardest lessons to learn was the importance of giving too few instructions. It took me a long time to learn this, and I am not sure even now that I have gone far enough. The urge to instruct, to tell people in detail how they should do something, is reinforced by being a teacher with a teacher's role to act out.

I began to learn this when I saw people doing things 'the wrong way'. The first time I saw matrix scoring I only knew about ranking, and nearly intervened to say, 'that's not the way to do it'. But matrix scoring has proved more versatile and discriminating than matrix ranking, which is now much less practised. There was a brilliant irony when it was my incompetence that made space for other people's creativity. This happened with a group of women on the slopes of Kilimanjaro in Tanzania, who matrix-scored 6 of the 13 varieties of banana they named. My limited Swahili prevented my telling them fully how to matrix-score out of 5 or 10 in each cell of the grid, so they did it their own way. They used free scoring, putting down a pile of maize grains for the score, and then counting them later. This was new to me and, as I came to understand, has its own special strengths. On top of that, instead of scoring them for a range of characteristics as I intended, their criteria for comparison were what mattered most to them, their suitability for different forms of cooking and food preparation. But I did not internalize the lesson at all well until at least a decade later when I began to learn not to give instructions in detail. At one time in PRA familiarization workshops I would spend half an hour 'teaching' matrix-scoring, with lots of dos and don'ts. Gradually I came to realize that two to three minutes could be enough;[1] that there was no single right way; and that people could learn and invent for themselves. 'The right way' is Newtonian, fixed, rigid, constraining. 'The wrong way' is open to emergence, the creative way, the way of discovering for oneself, the way of originality. Once the door was left open for 'the wrong way' I came to learn that there are at least a dozen ways in which matrix-scoring can be done.

13. Teasers

Teasing questions, asking people to guess, and betting some money on it, is a fun way of introducing variety and interest (PW: 110–11). Participants can be asked to guess almost anything. Especially potent are 'Whose Reality?' teasers. Any facilitator can make her own collection of these. Here is one of my favourites, which no one has ever guessed, but no doubt some one may in future if they read this.

Female sex workers on the Kenyan coast were asked what they would like that would make a difference to their lives. Can you guess one thing they said that was far from obvious? People guess condoms, respect, better accommodation, schools for their children, and so on. They do not guess this surprising thing: swimming lessons. Why? You have to ask them.

I love this one because quite apart from startling those who try to guess (a group of respectable, middle-class Liberal Democrats in my home town, Lewes, were flabbergasted, mystified and incredulous), it shows sex workers as people like other people.

14. Intentional silence *(Kaner et al., 1996: 53)*

This is a very powerful discipline for any facilitator. Quite simply, it entails saying nothing. Allowing time for others to think and speak. What in Latin America they call *suffrir il silencio*. It is painful and difficult to do but highly effective in enabling participants to think and express themselves.

Variants are senior silence, when all senior, or older, or male, or powerful people are not to speak. This is like the experts being 'on tap, not on top' (Gibson, 1996).

15. Fishbowl

Three to five chairs are arranged facing each other. Those who are to be empowered and enabled to speak, or whose views are sought, sit in the chairs facing one another. All others sit round and watch and listen, without saying anything. Those in the fishbowl can be students discussing their courses, or junior staff discussing their work, or other lowers, with their uppers sitting round.

Variants are many. One is that anyone can go and stand behind someone in the fishbowl, who will then, after having their say, retire and be replaced.

16. Neutralizing dominators *(see also PW: 180–7)*

Those who talk a lot in groups can have much to contribute that other group members appreciate; but they often do not give others much chance. This is often marked where some are very fluent and articulate in the language used, while others are not. There are many ways of neutralizing dominators or reducing their dominance, and/or making space for others to contribute:

- Stand behind the dominator and ask the group a question. The dominator then has to turn right round if they want to answer to you.
- Ask the dominator to facilitate the group and ensure that all have a chance to speak, if they wish to.
- Ask groups to identify who has been talking most and invite them to leave and form their own group.

17. Dragons and princesses

This is a great energizer (if somewhat politically incorrect). A woman student introduced this lively and hilarious energizer in a recent workshop (it is similar to 'Cats and Dogs' [PW: 39]). Two participants are dragons and the rest princesses. The dragons roar and open their arms like jaws, and chase the princesses. The princesses hop with their arms by their sides and hands out sideways, squealing loudly. (Rehearse and amplify the roars and squeals before starting.) When caught by a dragon a princess at once becomes a dragon and chases other princesses. This goes on until no princesses remain.

18. New gear

The most useful new gear of the past dozen years is the combination of parachute material (usually blue or green, expensive but very light, folds like a sari into almost nothing, and impossible to tear) and repositioning adhesive spray. Spray the material and fold sticky side to sticky. A good spray lasts from three to six uses. Put the material up on a wall. Cards can then be put on the material and easily moved around.

Tips
1. Keep the sticky surface clean. Blown sand (Shinyanga, Tanzania) can never be removed, nor dirt.
2. Use torn-up thin A4 paper for cards (A4 into thirds is good) as these are light, stick better than standard coloured cards in workshop kits, and do not make the material fall off the wall with their weight.
3. Use plenty of masking tape, or pins on pinboards, and exercise zero tolerance if the material falls down.
4. Discourage sticking on whole flip-chart sheets as these are liable to remove a good deal of the adhesive.

19. Walk round, review and talk–listen

I have found this a good sequence for finishing a day or a workshop. If there are enough walls, stick up workshop visuals and outputs in sequence as they are used or produced. Just before the end, the whole workshop can then be reviewed visually by walking around. This refreshes and reinforces memories and aids reflection on what has been done and learnt. Usually five to ten minutes is enough. Warn that talk–listen will follow. After the walk around for review and reflection, ask each participant to sit down with someone else. They take turns to talk while the other listens. What topics they cover is up to them – what has struck them, what they are taking away, what they disagreed with, what they are going to reflect on or do now. The listening is NOT active listening, which can be a bit forced, with listeners affirming what they are hearing with, 'What I am hearing you say is...'. It is just plain listening, not always easy to do and a good discipline in itself. Then after two or three minutes, speaker and listener switch roles. In this way everyone embeds some ideas by expressing them, and every-one hears what one other person has to say. After the second two or three minutes allow conversations to follow naturally without a deadline. The workshop can then dissolve without any formal end. Some leave at once. Others have animated conversations which can go on for 20 minutes or more. That is good.

20. Participatory workshops with large groups

There is a widespread belief that participatory workshops have to be with small or moderate numbers. This may come from the value placed on direct personal interaction between facilitator and participant. There may, too, be a sense that large numbers are daunting, which indeed they can be. But both these can be turned on their heads. Value can be placed on facilitating interactions between participants: these can be focused or structured in many ways. Large numbers can also be fun and even easier because the pressure is not always there to relate to individuals, but rather to manage a group process in which there can be a lot of buzzing (which can also be time off for the facilitator). Or so I rationalize to myself. There is ego there too, and though I don't want to say it, a bit of show-off pleasure in performance. Although each time I say, 'never again', once into it I am lost to myself; and activities we lose ourselves in tend to be fulfilling.

For whatever reasons and satisfactions, the fact is that large groups were more and more given to me. Workshops at IDS had to be at weekends because of scheduling problems between different course curricula and we wanted anyone to be able to come. Numbers have varied between 20 and 90, often around 40 or 50. The largest of all have been welcoming new students at the beginning of the academic year. The diversity and enthusiasm of the students have been a source of pleasure and inspiration. I would like others to know what can be done, so after this section, there follow 21 ways of welcoming and mixing very large groups.

21. Explore for yourself, try new ideas, improvise, invent and share your own

Twenty-one ways of welcoming, mixing and managing very large groups

For almost ten years we have been welcoming and mixing large groups of students who have just arrived for a year on a wide range of MA and MSc courses in development-related studies at the University of Sussex and the Institute of Development Studies. Typically they come from 20–25 countries and have about 35 different mother tongues. Numbers have varied between 100 and 150. The duration has been 0915 to 1300. The location has been two quite large rooms in IDS that can be joined by removing a divider, together with what was an extensive lawn outside until the University fenced much of it off for a pollination experiment.[2] Much of what follows comes from those workshops, and some from a Plan Zimbabwe annual retreat with 150 staff. Much has application not just for student welcomes, but for opening and welcoming conferences and other occasions with large numbers, and for smaller workshops.

The numbers and the diversity of participants present challenges and opportunities. In *Participatory Workshops* there is a relevant section, '21 ideas for participatory workshops with large numbers' (*PW*: 96–106). Large numbers there is taken to be 'around 30 or more people'. The ideas there are relevant but most of those which follow are new.

1. Negotiate and publicize the time

When people are coming from different organizations, courses, or parts of a college or university, negotiate a time of the greatest convenience to the greatest number. This may be weekends but that is liable to exclude many, such as parents with families (though children can be made welcome, can make it a more friendly occasion, and are often happy to sit and draw). Make sure the time and place are known to all well in advance. Give a start time 15 minutes before the time you really plan to start: while waiting, punctual people can meet one another, relax and look at materials.

2. Choose the space with care

Invest time in looking for a suitable space or spaces. Almost all the complaints about numbers being too large have really been about space being too small or lack of microphones. Search out a big space, including an outdoors lawn or courtyard if possible, to be used weather permitting. If it is cold, warn people to bring warm clothes.

3. Maximize the space

Find helpers, best the day before, but sometimes early arrivals on the day, to move tables to the walls, and stack chairs. Helpers rarely appreciate how much extra space can be made by collapsing tables or upending them on each other, or how chairs can be stacked and stowed. Some tables can be thought of for sitting on. Sometimes the furniture can be moved out of the room altogether. Allow for somewhere for people to put their impedimenta: underneath tables is often good.

4. Get good gear

Whatever is needed. A megaphone can be useful for outside and microphones for inside. Test them. Flip charts, flip-chart stands, big pens, a roll of sticky labels for name tags, and masking tape are usually essential.

5. On the day, be there early!

Often there is some emergency. I have been locked out and found the caretaker on leave! Tearing of hair. Or the room divider won't open. Or any one of a myriad of details needs sorting. I have rarely achieved the ideal of a relaxed facilitator greeting people as they arrive, but coming early does help.

6. On arrival

Put up a notice asking people to give themselves name tags for the name they like to be called, stow their gear away, and meet others. Sticky labels of the sort that come in rolls are good, and big pens. Make physical arrangements so that there is no queuing bottleneck.

7. Plan time and space use

Time: coffee/tea/biscuits in the middle of a morning are an important opportunity for people to meet one another. If there are fixed presentations to the whole group (a briefing about the library, about the environment, cycling and so on) they come best after a coffee break. Before a coffee break have activities that may need to run on into the break. Similarly at the end of a morning or afternoon.

Space: have tea and coffee in more than one place to reduce crowding. Avoid bottlenecks in movement. Maximize the width of any doors to be passed through. When passing through a door, challenge the group to go through in a fixed time, such as a minute.

8. Celebrate diversity

This can be done in many ways. Where there are many languages, one is a flip chart on which people can write a greeting or welcome in their language (and script where that applies).

9. Raise hands for silence

This is gentler and more effective than clapping for silence. Practise and establish this as a convention. As soon as one person raises a hand, others do too, and silence comes quickly.

10. Silent greetings

All walk around, weaving in and out of others, looking at the ground, and then successively greeting others with their eyes only, then their whole faces, their hands, a left or right elbow, a knee, a toe and then (male-to-male, female-to-female) their bottoms. A good icebreaker that ends in laughter.

11. Groups greet one another

Form small groups with identities. They then go round and meet and greet other groups. Nicely anarchic. If one group are hosts, let them form small groups; visitors too; and each host group walks over and meets and welcomes a visitors' group.

12. Stand on a map

A versatile, popular, informative and enjoyable icebreaker with any group, regardless of numbers. This is best outdoors in a big space. In a large area imagine north and give a point of reference, for example Nairobi, so that you can indicate where the equator goes. Each goes to their home country, or place within a country.

Tips. Tear up banners from flip charts in advance and ask participants to write their country's name in big letters, one banner per country, which can be held up. Personal migrations can be shown by moving around from place to place on the map. A megaphone can be useful. Remember that those behind may not be able to hear.

13. Mother tongues

Ask groups to form by mother tongue. Go round with the megaphone, let each shout out a greeting or similar in their mother tongue. Ask someone to count how many tongues there are, and then celebrate that.

14. Fractal circles

For groups of more than 50 this is better than bicycle chain (for which see PW: 22). Ask everyone to form two circles, one inside the other, and pair off. All then greet and shake hands (unless culturally/gender-insensitive), say the name of the other, and move to the left and repeat. When the circle has gone right round, the outer circle places their hands on their heads (i.e. they stay put) and the inner circle points to the sky (moves outside and reforms). Each circle then forms two new circles, pairs off, and repeats greetings and moves to the left. When this is complete, repeat and continue until the new groups are only about ten-strong, at which point they just greet one another anyhow. With a very large number the first and second rounds may have to be ended before they are complete. Not everyone meets everyone then, but it is not such a great loss.

Tips. Repeat the instructions twice using a flip-chart diagram. Limit the greeting – no conversations, but 'let's meet in the break' is acceptable. Tap shoulders in a fun way to unblock traffic jams – see who is responsible and jokingly warn them.

15. Buses

Cluster in groups by characteristics – the courses people are on, the gender proportions in each course, professional training, type of organization they come from or were in before coming. Sense whether to allow time for conversations to develop.

16. Meet opposites

Ask for groups of opposites, for instance, those more fluent and those less fluent in English, those knowing more and those knowing less about a subject. Groups of two or three are best, not more. Invite the opposites to pair off (for example, three women pair off with two men, or a more fluent speaker pairs off with two less fluent) and ask them to discuss their concerns about the year and issues around relationships. With students of varied fluency in the common language of a course (English, French, Spanish, Portuguese, Russian, Hindi, Chinese, etc.), ask the more fluent to be silent for the first two to three minutes and listen to those less fluent express the challenges they face and how they can be helped.

17. Feedback through write-up

If there is feedback from groups, have two, three or even four flip charts. As soon as they have a few points, each group sends someone to write them up while they continue. Any point already there can be ticked. This way all flip charts should be busy and queues minimized. This system maximizes participation and saves time. Immediate processing can be picking out a few key points. Volunteers can be asked to consolidate the lists and prepare a handout for later.

18. Feedback verbally in plenary

Ask each group in turn to say aloud one feedback item. Other groups raise their hands if they have it too. Volunteers count hands and write up the scores. Continue round the groups until there are no more contributions. Remark on those items most mentioned, and others perhaps relatively overlooked or surprising. With a group of more than a hundred, this is better and much faster than feedback through write-up, and all can hear what is being said.

19. Groups of maximum diversity

Ask participants to form groups of maximum diversity. Five is a good number. Let them define diversity for themselves. Give the groups a task. With student welcomes, this has been to tell the others why and how they have come, and their hopes, fears and expectations. A group of five typically takes about

25 minutes, and if they finish early continue with conversations. Plenary feedback is not needed.

20. Open space

When students have just arrived together and are meeting for the first time, this space can be for them to express their personal interests and meet others who share them. Those who wish may write their interest on a banner and display and parade it, attracting whoever they can. What will come up is unpredictable but hardy perennials include music, cooking, learning a language, jogging and dancing, with once, daringly, sex. Some groups have survived for a year. Open space is a good way to end a morning or afternoon because there is no sharp cut-off so it can go on for as long as participants wish.

21. Improvise

Invent your own tips and share what you do and learn. And of course ENJOY, because large groups can be a lot of fun.

Notes

1. I am not suggesting that this is always right. People complain that they need more instructions. Other trainers/facilitators take longer and get good results. Still, brief instructions fit the pattern that 'lowers' can discover and invent for themselves much more than uppers normally suppose.
2. I have nothing against pollination experiments, but this was a precious space for participatory workshops, teaching and learning; we have now lost in effect an outdoor classroom (weather permitting).

CHAPTER 6

Exploring the cogeneration of knowledge: critical reflections on PRA and CLTS

Sharing experience and cogenerating knowledge have been crucial in the development and spread of PRA (participatory rural appraisal) and CLTS (community-led total sanitation). The collective outputs of participatory workshops for sharing practices, innovations and experience have been part of wider networking and dissemination. They have generated ideas and evolved and agreed principles and good practices. Critical reflections concern power, planning and process, theory of change and impact, lessons learnt, and ongoing learning. The chapter concludes with 21 practical ideas for convening, conducting and following up on such participatory workshops.

Keywords: cogenerating knowledges, community-led total sanitation, critical reflection, emergence, participatory rural appraisal, participatory workshops, self-organizing systems on the edge of chaos, sharing and learning

Purpose and caveat

This chapter describes, analyses and draws practical conclusions from experiences with PRA[1] (participatory rural appraisal or participatory reflection and action) and CLTS[2] (community-led total sanitation) sharing and learning workshops. These workshops have common characteristics of purpose, context and methodology that may have wider application for the sharing and cogeneration of knowledge.

I have been exceptionally lucky to have had the freedom to be able to accompany PRA and CLTS in various contexts, countries and capacities. As an enthusiast, I am liable to have positive biases: in my view PRA and CLTS are enthralling in the potentials that they have opened up and continue to open up. I am also an academic sceptic interested in the truth and recognize that much practice in the name of PRA and CLTS has been, and remains, deeply flawed and must continuously be learnt from and improved upon. Memory is fallible (see e.g. Schulz, 2010), mine perhaps more than most. I have in part triangulated with written records and have tried to remember negative cases where approaches and methods have not worked, but my biases are still there. What follows is based on more than two decades of sharing and cogenerating

http://dx.doi.org/10.3362/9781780448220.006

workshops, perhaps a dozen on PRA from 1990 to about 1996, and more than a dozen on CLTS from 2009 to the present, mid-2013.

Context: the history of PRA and CLTS

PRA and CLTS are closely related participatory methodologies. While they have earlier roots, PRA has evolved since 1989 and CLTS since 2000. Many actors and organizations have been involved in many countries, with much diversity and creativity. Both PRA and CLTS have been and remain continuously evolving and spreading. The approach and methods of PRA have diffused into many other methodologies and practices. CLTS is a more specialized movement that has drawn on PRA tradition and practices.

PRA is often described as an approach and methods. The approach includes behaviour, attitudes and facilitating participatory analysis and action. The methods typically involve, but are not limited to, small groups of people doing their own analysis with visuals such as maps and diagrams on the ground or on paper. PRA was pioneered mainly in India in the very early 1990s, largely by Indians,[3] and by IIED[4] through training and innovating methods in many countries. PRA was quickly picked up by innumerable NGOs and also by governments. Results were mixed with some excellent practice and some mediocre or bad. PRA spread in the 1990s to over 100 countries, in at least 20 of which PRA networks were established. The IDS was generously and flexibly funded to support the sharing and spread of PRA, without the constraint of log frames and the like.

Applications of PRA methods have been innumerable (Chambers, 2008a: 301–2). People have made millions of participatory maps (social maps, resource maps, mobility maps, vulnerability maps and so on). Other methods such as pairwise ranking, matrix scoring, seasonal diagramming, wealth or well-being ranking, Venn or chapatti diagramming, and spider diagrams have been very widely used, and are a standard part of the repertoire of many government and NGO fieldworkers. Applications have been myriad, in many domains such as natural resource management, social protection, poverty appraisals, agriculture, health, women's empowerment, and HIV/AIDS.

CLTS is a more specialized participatory methodology. It springs from the PRA tradition. Rural community members are facilitated to face the facts of open defecation, often leading to their immediate decision to stop it. It was pioneered by Kamal Kar, a leading PRA trainer and practitioner, in Bangladesh very early in 2000. Through his efforts and initiatives of WSP (the Water and Sanitation Program of the World Bank), CLTS spread to India and then later with support from WSP, Plan International, WaterAid, UNICEF and other organizations, to over 50 other countries, at least 15 of which had (mid-2013) adopted it as part of their national strategy for rural sanitation. CLTS requires radical and difficult changes in policy and behaviour. Former policies of hardware subsidy for individual household latrines are abandoned: people dig and construct their own. Standard designs are discouraged: local designs take over. Achievement is no longer counted mainly as latrines constructed; it is communities credibly declared and verified as being open defecation free (ODF). The idea that poor and weak people need help from outside gives way to the idea that primary responsibility for helping them lies with and can be fulfilled by others in the community.

Enabling conditions

Seven conditions have enabled the spread of PRA and CLTS and have characterized the context in which sharing and cogenerating knowledge have occurred.

1. Grounded innovations that work

Both PRA and CLTS grew from and were evolved out of innovations with communities in real time. The methods and approach were cogenerated interactively with people. PRA exploded because visuals and group analysis worked. People in communities enjoyed making maps and representing their realities in diagrams. They showed and discovered for themselves that they were capable of far more complex representations and analysis than they or others had supposed; and these visuals proved versatile and useful in many contexts for many people for many purposes. CLTS has been similarly grounded. It, too, showed that people are capable of analysis and action that neither they nor outsiders had any idea of. It has simultaneously turned on their heads conventional ideas that poor rural people could not build their own latrines, had to be subsidized, and required a standard structure. Instead it relies on triggering awareness and action through facilitation: people are facilitated through CLTS exercises – they map their defecation areas, go and stand in them, calculate the volume of shit they produce, analyse for themselves the pathways of shit to the mouth, and so on – and are usually so disgusted when they conclude that they are 'eating one another's shit' that they decide to stop open defecation and often start digging pits at once.

2. Training, facilitation, scale and quality

From the very beginning it was evident with both PRA and CLTS that facilitation, and the attitudes, behaviours and relationships, of facilitators were central to success and to spread. The same has been found with other participatory methodologies (see Brock and Pettit, 2007; especially Nandago, 2007). Two very widespread international movements – Reflect (*Education Action*, 1994– continuing; Archer, 2007), which draws on both Freirean and PRA approaches, methods and traditions; and integrated pest management (IPM) (Pontius et al., 2002; Fakih et al., 2003) – both stress the critical importance of facilitators, their skills and behaviours. In Reflect, the facilitator is said to be the one in the group who talks least; in IPM it is said that you can tell the facilitator for he or she will be the first into the mud of the paddy field. In PRA and CLTS, training and mentoring have similarly been recognized as critical. Both PRA and CLTS have been subject to pressures to go fast to scale, and trainers and training organizations have popped up who lack vital orientations and abilities. Hands-on training in communities in real time has been crucial, but donors and governments eager to go to scale either have not known this or have ignored it, and much training has been not hands-on and experiential, but classroom-based. The mislearning, passed on from trainer to trainer, has then been counterproductive, sometimes tragically so on a vast scale.[5]

3. Flexible funding, institutions and trust

In their early days both PRA and CLTS were able to spread so dramatically because of donor understanding and flexibility. Funding for PRA reconnaissance and accompaniment in India in 1989–91 came from ODA (DFID/UKAid), the Ford Foundation and the Aga Khan Foundation. Originally work on participation in agricultural research was to have been a major part of the work I was funded for, but the donors gave me almost total freedom to follow the action where it led, which was to PRA. Throughout the 1990s, both IIED and IDS had flexible funding. Sida and SDC allowed IDS a substantial budget item for 'unanticipated opportunities' and were flexible about budget reallocations in the rapidly developing situation. There were no log frames. In the early 2000s this flexible funding was used to invite Kamal Kar to IDS to write his seminal working paper (Kar, 2003) that did so much to launch CLTS on the international scene. Between donors and IDS there was free and frank interchange, open communication, an advisory group chaired and facilitated by colleagues from developing countries, and an atmosphere of trust. Without that, CLTS could not have taken off as it did.

4. Champions, energy and action

Because they were grounded in interactive experience and disciplined by what worked in real time, both PRA and CLTS fired the enthusiasm of champions who then innovated and spread them. They sensed they were riding new waves with immense possibilities, but were also vulnerable to bad practice. The sharing and cogeneration of knowledge has then been driven not by academic analysis but by the energy and commitment of champions and practitioners with experience of what works and what does not work in practice.

5. Communities of commitment

Much has been written about communities of practice (COPs). What these may or may not have is commitment. It is almost a ritual now to set up a COP at the end of a successful workshop or conference. But on returning to their offices, participants are faced by many other priorities. Good intentions drown and die in a flood of emails. There is nothing to my knowledge that calls itself a community of practice with PRA and CLTS. What have evolved and been experienced are more than COPs. They are communities of collaboration, of mutual support, of solidarity, of shared inspiration, communities of commitment.

6. Face-to-face meetings

Throughout their histories, meetings and workshops have been a vital part of PRA and CLTS. Activists have come together face-to-face. Through meeting face-to-face people have got to know one another. The downside was the emergence of what others saw as a PRA in-group. The upside was continuity of learning, ease of communication and frank sharing between colleagues and friends. This has also been true of CLTS.

7. Communicating, networking and disseminating

Such actions have been continuous and pervasive. Early PRA involved networking and helping national networks to start, with encouragement and some small funds; this was led by John Thompson at IIED, and some of the networks such as NEPAN in Nepal and PAMFORK in Kenya survive to this day. IIED began as the global hub for the networks, but this then moved to Praxis in India, and then to the Centre for Development Services in Egypt. In contrast with PRA in the 1990s, for CLTS in the 2000s to the present, email and internet have made communicating and networking more instant and intense and have multiplied the scope for dissemination: innovations, reports, articles and blogs are continuously uploaded onto the CLTS website and a bimonthly newsletter with hyperlinks to new documents goes out to well over 3,000 recipients, still from the global CLTS knowledge hub in IDS. Perhaps in part because of the ease of communicating and sharing through the website there is no CLTS equivalent yet in the 2010s of the PRA national networks of the 1990s. Other activities include linking people together (such as CLTS trainers from Pakistan linked with training requests from Afghanistan), publications such as the CLTS Handbook (Kar with Chambers, 2008), and co-convening workshops. How these can be conducted has been improvised and invented on the run, providing raw material for the analysis that follows.

Participatory workshops for sharing and cogenerating knowledge

Participatory workshops for sharing and cogenerating knowledge have played an important part in the development and spread of both methodologies. They have involved, and with CLTS continue to involve, practitioners, activists, engaged academics and others. With CLTS in India they regularly include community members known as Natural Leaders.

These workshops have been deeply influenced by the methodologies with which they have been concerned. Cogeneration is in the genes of PRA and CLTS. Both methodologies were discovered and evolved through explorations and innovations in and with people in rural communities. Both were born and grew in real life, hands-on situations through interactions with community participants who (Chapter 4, first section) astonished outsiders with what they could do. With PRA they showed how PRA processes take off and facilitation is not only then not needed, but can be a distraction. An outsider facilitator can observe and assess but usually does best during group-visual activities to keep quiet and be inconspicuous. People then make visible and cogenerate their own knowledge. For more on this and its rigour, see *Whose Reality Counts? Putting the First Last* (Chambers, 1997: 117–61). So it was too with CLTS but with the difference that CLTS facilitation is more interventionist, more specific to sanitation and hygiene, and it has in the minds of the facilitator a hoped-for outcome in the form of a community decision to totally sanitize itself. Participation and cogeneration remain at the core of both methodologies and families of methods.

Types and contexts of cogenerating workshops

With PRA and CLTS, these cogenerating workshops have been of six types.

1. Immersion workshops

Immersions are a form of experiential learning in which the learner stays and lives for some days and nights in a community: living with them, working with them, wandering around and experiencing their lives (Eyben, 2004; Irvine et al., 2004; PLA, 2007; Birch and Catani, 2007). In the early 1990s, three South–South sharing workshops in India included participants from other continents for immersions and PRA practice in Indian villages, a tradition continued by Jimmy Mascarenhas and his organization Outreach. Immersions tend to be intense and memorable. It is standard good practice to process the experiences of immersions individually and collectively, with facilitated critical reflection and learning shared mutually with host families and other participants. Numbers have usually been between 1 and 20.

2. Training workshops and learning and innovating through training

These have been hands-on in real time in communities. The PRA workshops of the early and mid-1990s convened and facilitated by IIED and to a lesser extent IDS, and the CLTS training workshops of Kamal Kar and others, from the early and mid-2000s onwards (Kar, 2010) have had this character, which has made them occasions also for innovation. IIED trainers were continuously experimenting, trying out new ideas, improvising on the run, finding what worked, and pushing the limits to see what local people were capable of, as were many others in India and elsewhere. Learning through training is a phrase sometimes used. Innovating through training goes further, not just in how trainings are done, but substantive innovation in the hands-on activities themselves. Numbers have usually been between 20 and 60.

3. Critical issue and topic workshops

With PRA, three international workshops broke new ground by confronting urgent issues facing PRA: one in IDS in 1994 (Kumar, 1997b), and two in India, in Bangalore (Kumar, 1996) and Kolkata (Kumar, 1997a). Then an international group was convened in 2000 to reflect critically on PRA, leading to the book *Pathways to Participation* (Cornwall and Pratt, 2003). Other workshops also led to other books (see below). With CLTS topic workshops have begun to tackle and consolidate experience as needs and priorities have emerged, including School-Led Total Sanitation, and Going to Scale with Quality (Lukenya Notes). A variant has been the writeshop in which practitioners and others meet with their drafts, together with editors, and cooperate, critiquing each other's work and redrafting. A CLTS writeshop held in Kenya, co-convened and facilitated jointly by IDS, IIED and Plan Kenya, led in 2010 to Petra Bongartz, Angela Milligan and Samuel Musyoki editing *Tales of Shit: Community-Led Total Sanitation in Africa* (Participatory Learning and Action 61). Numbers in topic workshops have usually been between 10 and 60.

4. Regular collegial meetings

In the UK, throughout the first half of the 1990s, numerous, often monthly, workshops took place in IDS with colleagues from IIED and others, with sharing and brainstorming, which built up a powerful community of collegiality. With CLTS the IDS hub initiated and convenes meetings of a UK CLTS Action and Learning Group of colleagues in other organizations involved with CLTS for very informal sharing of information and ideas on CLTS, hosted at different times by IDS, Plan, WaterAid and DFID. Numbers have usually been between 10 and 20.

5. Research project workshops

For the CLTS research and action learning research project led by Lyla Mehta there was a workshop in India for partners to meet and plan, and a final workshop in IDS for the presentation of findings, later published as *Shit Matters* (Mehta and Movik, 2011). Numbers were in the order of 30–40.

6. Regional workshops

CLTS regional workshops have been co-convened in South-east Asia (with Plan, UNICEF, WSP and others), Eastern and Southern Africa (Mombasa with Plan), anglophone Africa (Lusaka with Plan and UNICEF), francophone

West Africa (Bamako with UNICEF), and India (Nainital, Shimla (twice)), and Gurgaon with variously the CLTS Foundation, the Key Resource Centre Nainital, the Government of India, and the governments of Himachal Pradesh and Haryana. Other regional workshops have been one-day affairs on the eve of main continental biennial sanitation conferences such as AfricaSan, SacoSan (South Asia) and LatinoSan. Many contacts and links have resulted, together with much South–South meeting and collaboration. Numbers have been between 30 and 120.

Common dimensions of sharing and cogenerating

Though differing in numbers, duration and context, these workshops have common characteristics.

Knowledges

Knowledge as a singular noun is unitary. There is or should be one knowledge. This is latent and implicit in much conventional science. In reality, there are many knowledges – indigenous, technical, scientific, individual, contextual and so on. Those who take part in sharing and cogenerating workshops bring their own knowledges, some of which overlap, and some of which are personal in the form of methods, approaches and experiences they know about and others do not. Through sharing, interacting, brainstorming, provoking ahhas! and new insights, new knowledges are generated. What comes out of such a workshop is then more than a sum of the knowledges brought to it. To the extent that it is captured or expressed in a written output it can be described, as I have done so far in this chapter, in its singular form, as a knowledge, while participants still have their personal knowledges, now modified and perhaps enriched.

Power

Power is exercised before, during and after workshops. Before workshops there is convening power: the power to determine and articulate the topic, to decide who to invite (with powers of inclusion and exclusion), to choose the venue and to plan the programme. During a workshop there is the power exercised by facilitators and others to influence the process, the agenda and the sorts of knowledges that are shared and generated. There is power in the hands of those who draft and write up. Later there is dispersed power to disseminate, influence and follow up. Inclusive participatory attitudes, behaviours and practices can inform all of these. The various powers can be used well or otherwise.

Tensions and paradoxes: planning versus emergence

Frequent tensions before workshops are demands for the comfort of a clear agenda and programme, but this conflicts with the knowledge that, with the participatory emergence of sharing and cogenerating, whatever we planned would not be what happened. To be sure, field trips must be arranged in advance, and excursions for shopping and the like, and if there are outside visitors (though it may be best to avoid the distraction they can be), the times of their visits may have to be fixed. Demands for a preset programme may have to be humoured. To maintain flexibility, one device is to leave time open, labelling a section 'Open Space'.

Outputs

Paradoxically, planning to have some outputs, such as a consensus statement, may reduce the chances of it happening. Too much preparation and planning can constrain, conflicting with the principle of optimal unpreparedness. Some of the best outputs have flowed unpredictably from process and the coalescence of a sense that a statement of some sort would be right and feasible. A factor contributing to this is how participants come to know and respect one another, and how they find interactions and exchanges enjoyable and informative. This is part of an emergent workshop atmosphere or culture, which cannot be assumed or assured in advance. Indeed, the chemistry may be such that it does not come about.

In one workshop where the intention to have an agreed statement at the end was announced up front, it proved out of the question. In both Lusaka and Bamako, had we announced at the outset that we were aiming for a declaration or statement of consensus, I think it would have been less likely; or if it had come about it would have taken longer and been less comprehensive and forceful. An exception was the Nainital Statement (April 2013) when the Government of India wanted a statement to contribute to reformulating national policy for rural sanitation[6] and the workshop was oriented towards that; though with normally predictable unpredictability the participatory process overflowed (with lunch at 1600) and the Statement had to be drafted the day after the workshop.

Preliminary process

Precisely where the programme has evolved flexibly, adapting to energy, interest and flow, workshops have been most creative and productive. While there are and should be many variants (each workshop process is unique), certain activities have been common, with four as fairly basic.

1. Preliminaries to establish mutual understanding, including so-called icebreakers and informality. This and other good workshop practices will not be laboured here, but are fundamental in setting the tone and nurturing a friendly and open culture and practices.
2. Facilitation and confirmation of a collective overall purpose.

3. Individuals or small groups writing on cards the issues or topics to be tackled. Sorting of the cards (usually on the floor) into emergent categories.
4. Either in plenary or groups, sharing, debating, brainstorming and agreeing on the issues or topics.

This process has several advantages. All participants are able to contribute their ideas. It does not take long. It establishes a consensus agenda at the start. In a South Asia PRA three-day workshop retreat at Thakani in Nepal, this whole process took half an hour and established an agenda which worked well for the three days.

SOSOTEC: self-organizing systems on the edge of chaos

(See also page 116)

SOSOTEC can follow on naturally from the preliminary process or can be introduced later. It can be thought of as a proactive variant on Open Space (Owen, 2008). It worked well, for example, in the workshop that led to *Pathways to Participation* (Cornwall and Pratt, 2003) when adopted unplanned and on the run. While to a neo-Newtonian mindset this will appear disorganized and messy, it belongs in a paradigm of complexity and adaptive pluralism (Chambers, 2010). Simple rules, in this case facilitated activities, driven by the energy of adaptive agents, in this case participants, can be very productive in giving rise to unforeseeable results.

A SOSOTEC process can be designed to elicit and collect knowledges, leading to written outputs. The first full example I know of was the international ABC (attitude and behaviour change) workshop held in Bangalore and Madurai in 1996 (Kumar, 1996). Partly based on card writing and sorting, seven categories of topic emerged, and participants volunteered as pairs to be recorders and hunter-gatherers for those deemed highest priority. Each pair set up a station with a laptop in a different part of the room. Anyone could contribute anywhere at any time. Some went off and had intense discussions. Others were pulled in to make contributions. Remarkably, 18 participants in the heat of the moment wrote down their personal experiences of attitude and behaviour change (a riveting and revealing read). One went off for three hours and drafted 'Sharing our experience: An appeal to donors and governments', which was then discussed, amended and signed by all participants. In 36 hours in which the energy was such that some had little sleep, the substance of a small book (Kumar, 1996) was written and it remains in wide circulation.

SOSOTEC for a written output has since been used several times (see page 116). It is vulnerable to participants who question the process (though they usually come to accept and appreciate it), or who would prefer everything in plenary, or who lack relevant knowledge, experience or commitment. Participants may also take on writing without the necessary aptitude or competence. Failure to complete drafting once meant that a key chapter of a book had to be abandoned: the would-be author who had collected and been given excellent material simply failed to deliver. It is important that a capable editor taking part in the workshop has time available immediately after a SOSOTEC. Without this there can be a long delay. In sum, SOSOTEC is not a magic wand. When it works well, it can be brilliant. But success cannot be taken for granted. It is sensitive to energy, commitment, capabilities and a sense of common purpose.

Knowledges, theory of change and impacts

Written outputs – books, agreed statements and reports – are the main tangible medium in which knowledges generated in workshops are captured and expressed. A common theory of change is that these will be read and used and influence policy and practice. Books following PRA and CLTS workshops include *The Myth of Community: Gender Issues in Participatory Development* (Guijt and Shah, 1998); *Whose Voice?* (Holland with Blackburn, 1998); *Who Changes?* (Blackburn with Holland, 1998); *Stepping Forward: Children and Young People's Participation in the Development Process* (Johnson et al., 1998); *Pathways to Participation* (Cornwall and Pratt, 2003); *Springs of Participation* (Brock and Pettit, 2007); and *Shit Matters* (Mehta and Movik, 2011) (an output of a research project at the end of which there was a workshop). Agreed documents from early PRA were the 1994 statement about PRA (Absalom et al., 1995) from an IDS workshop, and *The ABC of PRA* (Kumar, 1996) from Bangalore and Madurai. Consensus statements from CLTS workshops have been from Nainital (2009) (one page, and subsequent four-pager); The Lusaka Declaration (2010) (seven pages); The Bamako Consensus (2010) (14 pages); Lukenya Notes on Going to Scale with Quality (2011) (72 pages); and the Nainital Statement (2013) (two pages). These and some of their predecessors may be of interest for process, methodology and relevance to practice and policy.

We – convenors, facilitators and participants in these workshops – have shared the common aim of wanting to make a difference, most of all in taking PRA and CLTS to scale with quality and sustainability. Our implicit theory of change has been that if we bring together our experience and ideas and converge on a practical consensus, this can be influential. As I review the written outputs it is striking how practical and policy-oriented they are. This shows more in the statements than the books. With the books there are time lags, often two or more years, the content tends to be more descriptive and analytical than prescriptive, and the writing is discursive with paragraphs and chapters. If they have impacts, they are long-term. The reports of PRA workshops – *The ABC of PRA* (Kumar, 1996) and *PRA – Going to Scale: Challenges for Training* (Kumar, 1997a) – are intermediate between statements and books but were produced in a matter of weeks and have many recommendations. The statements and shorter outputs of CLTS differ even more sharply from the books. They have been written and agreed during the workshops or very soon afterwards, and they have been heavily prescriptive. They contain introductory texts but are often organized and presented as a series of bullet points.

But what impact have these had? It is hard to know. The statements have been immediately put on the first page of the CLTS website. Their hyperlinks have been in the bimonthly newsletter, received at their request by over 4,000 people. However, in our world of overcommunication there has to be a nagging question about how much they are read, referred to, accepted, internalized and acted upon.

One set of impacts has, however, been clearer. It is on and through participants. Those of us who experienced these workshops learnt and internalized a lot. By the end we have learnt much from each other and from the synergies of brainstorming that generate new insights and knowledge. We can feel we own the outcomes, and the consensual process generates commitment to them and enthusiasm.

We learn too from disagreement and debate. The most contentious and difficult issues can tell us much: in Lusaka they concerned field allowances for both NGO and government staff and rewards to communities, leaders and Natural Leaders; in Bamako it was the timing and extent of training masons, which if too early could slow implementation and block villagers' creativity; in Nainital it was whether incentive payments after communities had been verified open defecation free should be paid to individuals or to communities as a whole. With these and many other issues, the negotiated and agreed outcomes could be used by participants at once to confront the problems they faced. More generally, a number of participants, probably a majority, used the statements immediately in meetings and workshops on their return to their countries or in India to their States.

Attributing policy impacts is problematic for well-known reasons. The Lukenya Notes cite three cases where African governments had faced down donors and lenders who were pushing the policy of individual household subsidy, which impedes and even prevents CLTS. Ghana with the World Bank, Chad with the EU, and Nigeria over a period of months with the African Development Bank, had all managed to do this. Through the Lukenya process and Notes this was known in Mauritania, when it renegotiated successfully the terms of a subsidy-based project funded by the African Development Bank. It would be gratifying to attribute this to the Notes but reportedly the main factor was the Minister's convictions about CLTS based on his field visits. With the first Nainital workshop, there was a one-pager agreed in plenary, and a four-pager written the next day and these were used for a policy workshop in Delhi. With the second Nainital workshop there was a Government of India request for a short statement, some of which went to the highest policy level. But as ever, attribution of policy impact remains conjectural.

Lessons learnt from participatory methodologies

We can now ask what have we learnt about sharing and cogenerating knowledges, based on experiences with PRA and CLTS, which might apply to participatory methodologies (PMs) more widely?

From the point of view of a base or hub, wherever it is situated, that seeks to support the development of a PM and its spread with quality, this can be answered at two levels. The first is about principles and practices. The second is the twenty-one more specific do- and don't-type lessons for participatory sharing and cogenerating workshops which follow below.

The principles and practices that follow are suggestions, not imperatives, and are not set in stone: in the spirit of action learning, everything is open to questioning and improvement.

- Use action learning and networking as umbrella terms to describe the synergistic activities of evolving and sharing participatory methodologies. Action learning includes giving space, opportunity and occasion for practitioners and trainers to brainstorm, to record and exchange their experiences, and through interactions to go further in generating new knowledges and ideas. Networking includes a multiplicity of activities of linking, communicating and dissemination.
- Pursue many activities in parallel and try to optimize links and synergies between them, each contributing to others. Examples from CLTS are a website, a newsletter, writing, synthesizing, publication, translations, videos, blogs, workshops, country visits, email exchanges, others' research and publications, with many cross-links.
- Develop personal face-to-face relationships with champions and back them and put them in touch with one another.
- Listen to and learn from critics but do not let this absorb too much of your time and energy. I have been criticized for not replying to some criticisms. But time and energy have opportunity costs. At the margin, examples and learning from what works and does not work may make more difference for the better than further academic debate.
- Encourage and support leading trainers and practitioners to go freelance and become full time, while warning them of the dangers.
- Share without boundaries while trying to ensure quality in going to scale.
- Accept blame where justified, but aim and hope that others will take ownership and credit. When they do so, consider this success. With ownership comes commitment, energy, resources, innovation, local fit and much more potential learning.
- Encourage and support other networks, as feasible and appropriate, with a view to phasing out your own activities.
- Try to ensure flexibility in your budget. Unexpected opportunities can be expected. They have always occurred. Kamal Kar's initial visit to IDS to write his seminal 2003 working paper on CLTS was possible because of the flexible funding we had then in IDS. Without that launch pad, CLTS could not have taken off as fast or as well as it did. Imprisoned by their frameworks, donors no longer allow that flexibility. It would be heavy-handed to underline the irony.

- Convene and especially co-convene workshops. Persuade co-convenors to leave much of the agenda open.[7] As we have seen, such workshops have been key occasions for sharing experiences, co-learning and brainstorming to co-evolve insights and practical lessons.

Final reflections

In workshops, practices, experiences, ideas and principles become clearer to those who articulate them. At the same time they cross-fertilize and grow. Acts of articulation and interactions of sharing, learning from and with each other, brainstorming and reflecting combine to generate new knowledge. Expressing knowledges, experiences or ideas becomes a creative process that gives them form. But it matters what sort of form they take and how this is treated. If the form is bounded and fixed like a physical thing, and more so if it is defended like a territory, there is less scope for subsequent learning. If the form is more tentative and open-ended, and subject to continuing critical reflection and change, learning can be ongoing and evolutionary. At their best, this is what workshops provide conditions for and facilitate.

This conclusion has then itself to be open-ended, pluralist and tentative. Adding activities to the repertoire that development professionals are comfortable to use, and affirming good ones already known, is more important than trying to define a cohesive new approach with a sharp identity. Let this then end with quotations from the consensus statement (Absalom et al., 1995) of one of the earliest PRA workshops: 'PRA practitioners have come to stress personal behaviour and attitudes, role reversals, facilitating participation through group processes and visualization, critical self-awareness, embracing error and sharing without boundaries. ... We offer this statement of principles in the hope that others will share their experience, views and values in the same spirit so that we can all continue to learn from each other.'

That is the spirit of this chapter, and I hope it will encourage others to share, criticize and contribute so that together we can continue to find more ways to do better.

Twenty-one ideas for activities for participatory workshops for sharing and cogenerating knowledge

These ideas come from PRA and CLTS sharing, learning and cogenerating workshops. So that it can stand alone as a practical guide, it includes some of the points made above. Most of these workshops have been international. Most of the tips may have wider relevance, but readers will judge. See also *Participatory Workshops: A Sourcebook of 21 Sets of Ideas and Activities* (Chambers, 2002), referred to below as PW. In the tradition of those 21s, here are twenty-one sets of tips, based on practical lessons I think we have learnt. They are organized in three sections: A Planning and preparation; B The workshop; C Follow-up and actions.

A Planning and preparation

1. *Reflect on the why? of the workshop and the so what? at the end.* What sort of workshop is it? What sorts of knowledges are you hoping will be shared, learnt about and cogenerated? What are the expectations and hopes of others? Is it intended to contribute to policy or to practice? Who might co-convene and co-facilitate? Who has what (including creativity) to share? Who can contribute to the content of the workshop and to its process and culture? Who needs to meet whom? How will participants benefit? Who will any outputs be for? Who will be able and willing to follow up in preparing, disseminating and further developing outputs? What outputs, follow-up and impact should the workshop have?

2. *Write or co-create a concise concept note.* Do not make this long lest it constrain flexibility and scope for changing agenda and direction and seizing opportunities. Send the note out with invitations. For the more creative workshops say that you expect the process to evolve and that the concept, agenda and purpose may develop.

3. *Use workshops to get to know key players face-to-face.* There is no full alternative to meeting face-to-face. Skype, teleconferences and group telephone conversations are not a substitute, though they are more effective when you have already met face-to-face. The group immersions in villages of the first PRA South–South, combined with the early PRA workshops, gave many of us a sense of common identity, and we liked and respected one another. The numerous joint IIED-IDS workshops of early PRA helped us share and reinforce excitement and solidarity. They were occasions to look forward to. With CLTS, the WSSCC (Water Supply and Sanitation Collaborative Council) Global Forum in Mumbai in September 2011 gave some of us a sense of reunion, almost of family, as we met again people we already knew from earlier regional sanitation conferences or other contexts. The sense of common purpose and relationships that can result is precious.

4. *Co-convene.* Some workshops cannot and should not be co-convened, but co-convening has much to be said for it: it means co-commitment and co-ownership, brings in wider experience to decision-making, often shares costs, and improves chances of follow-up. One, two or at most three partners may be optimal. With more partners, transaction costs rise if they engage with the preparatory process, exponentially for each additional partner. This happened when we had five or six partners for a South-east Asia regional CLTS workshop in Pnom Penh, with a blizzard of widely copied emails.

5. *Choose a fitting venue.* The venue should match the occasion, the participants and the purpose. This is easier said than done. For a participatory workshop, the usual conditions of space, furniture, wall

space and equipment apply (see page 85). Relative isolation, peace and good amenities matter for writeshops, and for sharing and brainstorming workshops that have the character of retreats. (An ideal venue is the Lukenya Getaway near Nairobi where the Lukenya Notes were hatched and the *Tales of Shit* writeshop was held.) I think one reason why Nepan (The Nepal Participatory Action Network) has survived for almost 20 years is that the founders had two or three quiet retreats outside Kathmandu to reflect, evolve and agree basic principles, and plan and decide how to establish it. At the other extreme, where ministers and senior officials are involved, it may be (but not necessarily is) advisable to move upmarket for the venue. Proximity to field visits matters, though (see point 15 below) longish journeys can be turned to good uses.

6. *Plan but do not overplan.* Distinguish fixed points from open time. Fixed points may be the start, an opening if there has to be one, the end and closing if there has to be one, field visits, and shopping or tourist time off. Then plan backwards with cards on the floor. List topics and activities on cards. Start planning with how you intend to end. Then add fixed points. Then continue planning backwards, inserting and moving the cards around. Recognize rhythm and anticipate low points – usually at or just over half time – Wednesday afternoon in a five-weekday workshop. In such a workshop Wednesday is a good day for a field trip or an afternoon off or doing something different.

7. *Be prepared and optimally unprepared with the programme.* Government people and some others often want a detailed programme. When there has to be a formal opening or closing this is more needed than when there is not. The degree of pre-programming depends on the nature of the workshop. It is quite often politic to have a programme even though you know it will in the event not be followed. Be careful though if there are people coming for only one or a few sessions, as they may arrive to find you doing something else. One device is to label sessions, or half a day, or a whole day, or even more, as OPEN SPACE. This has the advantage of a meaning which is both specific (PW: 125–6), giving legitimacy, and general, giving flexibility. Optimal unpreparedness means being open to an unfolding process that cannot be fully foreseen. Where possible avoid giving a closing time for the day – a good participatory process can stimulate energy, excitement and commitment that often should run its course into late afternoon and evening.

8. *Be careful and thorough with invitations.* Some of those I invited to the first PRA South–South lacked relevant experience or were unable to follow up. It was a wasted opportunity. The 'wrong' people can also be a distraction. On the other hand, and more important, failure to invite key people who should be invited, or who feel they should, can cause lasting resentment, damaging if those slighted harbour a grudge. Be careful to inform and

invite people in the host country, city or area. Issue invitations well in advance if you can. Avoid difficult times of year, such as just before the end of the financial year. This can matter a great deal with governments and government people.

9. *Be aware of government protocol.* When inviting individual named government people, getting procedure and process right can be time-consuming and frustrating. Unless government is a sponsor or co-convenor, assuring good government participation can require care and patience. Sometimes a person you want to invite can give informed advice on how to proceed.

10. *Act early for visas.* It is sad how often late applications for visas prevent participation in international workshops and conferences. Ease of obtaining visas may even be a necessary factor in choice of country for the venue. Some countries have few embassies in other countries, which can delay, complicate and add to the financial and transaction costs of getting visas.

11. *Identify key documents, encourage participants to study them in advance and have them available.* There may be research reports or summaries, websites or other documents. Do not overload invitees but ensure that they are informed and up to date. Where government policy is involved identify and make available key policy statements and other documents.

B The workshop

12. *Encourage multiple ownership and credit.* Do not seek a high profile or institutional or personal recognition. Let ownership and credit be collective. Any impression that a workshop is a PR exercise for an organization is damaging and self-defeating. Do not allow yourself big ideas about your own importance.

13. *Set an informal atmosphere, and err on the side of informality.* There are several ways of setting the atmosphere at the beginning (PW: 5–30). For CLTS, Kamal Kar's 'greet others and tell them when you last did a shit in the open' works well. Standing on a map and then making brief self-introductions is another good way. In India we used it in the first Nainital workshop with mainly government people when waiting for the arrival of the VIP for the formal opening, and in Gurgaon after the opening with about 60 people. It is acceptable to senior people – Principal Secretaries in Tanzania were delighted and found it fun and interesting. Buses is another – at AfricaSan in Kigali clustering by type of organization provoked an instant animated buzz which ran on for almost 10 minutes as government people met government people from other countries, and the same for separate clusters of people from international agencies, INGOs and NGOs, and one group for freelancers.

14. *Brainstorm to create the agenda.* This applies mainly with smaller workshops, with say 10–50 participants, but was also part of the second Nainital workshop with over 100 participants. A concept note, or a sense of common purpose, and a framework of timings may already exist. The agenda can come from all participants brainstorming and/or individually writing on cards, which are then sorted on the ground into emergent categories. These can then be discussed and agreed. The clustered cards can provide the basis for plenary or group activities. In a PRA sharing workshop in Pakistan seven topics coalesced. Three were crosscutting. So four groups were formed, and each included in their agenda each of the three that crosscut. In several cases the clusters of cards have provided the structure for a final practice and policy output – *The ABC of PRA* (Kumar, 1996), the Lusaka Declaration (2010), the Bamako Consensus (2010), Lukenya Notes (2011), the Lilongwe Briefings (2012) and the Nainital Statement (2013).

15. *Make good use of car and bus journeys!* Car and bus journeys are opportunities. In Zambia we had a four-hour bus journey from Lusaka to visit Chief Macha's ODF (Open Defecation Free) Chiefdom. During the trip back we moved around and discussed. Out of those conversations came the idea of the Lusaka Declaration. Without the consensus and commitment that developed from interactions during that bus trip this would not have happened. With smaller vehicles, you can change seats and have long conversations with different people on different legs of the journey. An advantage of vehicles is the lack of eye contact and the lack of pressure to keep talking, allowing time for reflection.

16. *SOSOTEC.* (See also pages 108–9). In cases of SOSOTEC (self-organizing systems on the edge of chaos) (PW: 93, 103, 105, 116, 123–8) it is best not to be pre-programmed. Brainstorming onto cards and sorting them sets a starting agenda (as in point 14 above). Volunteers come forward to be champions (often for clusters of cards to which they have contributed). Ideally there will be two or three champions for each subject. Between them they combine and take turns as writers, interviewers, recorders, searchers and hunter-gatherers for their topic. Each topic group sets up shop with table/s, chairs and laptop/s, together with their cards. They plan their activities, and then work as a team to tap into their own knowledges, experience and ideas, and to solicit those of others. The process then runs itself. Forms of SOSOTEC contributed to *The ABC of PRA* (Kumar, 1996), *Springs of Participation* (Brock and Pettit, 2007), the Lusaka Declaration (2010) and the Bamako Consensus (2010), and were key to Lukenya Notes (2011).

17. *Declare a PowerPoint-free zone.* PowerPoint did not seriously raise its head until the 2000s. Now, unless warned in advance, participants are liable to prepare presentations in advance and feel hurt if they cannot show and

speak to them. 'Death by PowerPoint' is now a cliché. PowerPoint can slow and stop a participatory process: it is preset, inflexible, interrupts flow, takes time (often more than allocated), induces passivity and cannot easily respond to emergence. Very selectively and sparingly used it can be positive, especially with visuals – in presenting one or a very few photographs or key diagrams. However, to avoid its damaging distractions, we have repeatedly declared in advance that workshops will be PowerPoint-free zones (the first Nainital, Lusaka, Bamako, Kigali, Lukenya).

18. *Use Participatory PowerPoint (PPP)* (PW: 139–40) Contradicting point 17 above, PPP is a brilliant and quick way of achieving agreement and consensus on a text. A fast and accurate typist familiar with the topic sits and writes, with the text projected on a screen for all to see. The text can be composed jointly, or usually better and faster as a draft, which is then modified. Proposed changes can be entered in italics, and then changed to normal when agreed. If there is a serious debate or a deep disagreement, text can be abandoned, or a small group delegated to go off and hammer out a revision and bring it back. Without PPP we could never have achieved the Lusaka Declaration or the Bamako Consensus, which largely solved the problem of a back-to-office report for participants, and gave them a potent tool with the legitimacy of international consensus for changing policy and practice at home.

C Follow up and actions

19. *Think in advance about follow-up and seek agreement on actions.* Follow-up needs to be planned for but announcing it up front may be undermining. Ideally ideas and commitments emerge from the participatory process and come individually and collectively from participants. Far too often follow-up is lacking. Either it is promised and does not happen, or at the end of a workshop, particularly if there has to be a formal closing, discussing it is squeezed out of by lack of time. Follow-up on a lot of text, as with the Lukenya workshop on going to scale with quality, can involve time-consuming editing and iterations with drafts. Plan ahead and agree that someone will have the time.

20. *Ensure short, prompt summaries of workshops and short, punctual reports.* A succinct record quickly produced and widely circulated can be useful and have an impact. Longer reports circulated later are rarely read. The sad syndrome is that laborious notes are taken, maybe by students unfamiliar with the topic, then written up blow by blow to become a non-event scanned only by those who want to see if their valuable contributions are mentioned. Avoid this. Go for a short, punchy summary of main points. Pre-plan for this, ring-fencing time immediately after a workshop. The first Nainital workshop had a one-page statement agreed by the workshop, and a four-page summary written the next day – these being inputs to a

follow-up meeting of about 70 people in Delhi three weeks later. The two-page Nainital Statement from the second Nainital workshop was written the day after, sent to participants for comment, and adopted as final within a few days. Lukenya Notes were different: we did not plan for an executive summary but two people volunteered to produce one, and it is that summary that will receive the most attention, while at the same time pointing to the topics in the main text.

21. *Convene or co-convene in your own way, and share what you do and learn.*

Notes

1. For PRA, see Chambers, 1994 and 1997; and Cornwall and Pratt, 2003. It is sometimes renamed Participatory Reflection and Action. See also <www.participatorymethods.org>.
2. For CLTS, see Kar, 2003; Kar and Pasteur, 2005; Kar with Chambers, 2008; Bongartz and Chambers with Kar, 2009; Kar, 2010; Mehta and Movik, 2011; and <www.communityledtotalsanitation.org>.
3. Notably including Jimmy Mascarenhas and his team, and Sam Joseph, Parmesh Shah, Anil Shah, Meera Kaul Shah, Sheelu Francis, Somesh Kumar, Neela Mukherjee, Kamal Kar, John Devavaram, Ravi Jayakaran, Prem Kumar, Vidya Ramachandran and others, with early support from MYRADA and ActionAid.
4. Notably Jules Pretty, Irene Guijt, Ian Scoones and John Thompson.
5. With PRA an example was the Indian Watershed Programme of the mid-1990s with its cascade training of hundreds of trainers in a few months. With CLTS examples have been earlier cascade training in Nigeria and Tanzania.
6. <www.communityledtotalsanitation.org/resource/nainital-statement-national-workshop-community-led-approach-context-nirmal-bharat-abhiyan>
7. Unfortunately this is easier said than done. Co-convenors have repeatedly demanded a timetable which we well know will have to be abandoned.

PART III

Into the new unknown

CHAPTER 7

Exploring for our faster future world

Critical explorations and passionate communities are means for rapid learning and adapting in our world of accelerating change. The new duality of realities – virtual and physical/social – is getting out of balance. Exploring through experiential learning in the physical and social worlds remains fundamental for opening up ways of living and being that are effective, fulfilling and fun. We can all enjoy being explorers.

Keywords: accelerating change, being, communities of passion, critical explorers, digital tyranny, dual realities (virtual and physical/social), experiential learning, futures, living, white water, who gains? who loses?

So where do the experiences and reflections in this book take us? Has this been simply a transparent ego trip? Or are there lessons for our future, and for how we approach that future and live in it? Is there a danger of idealizing the experiences described, and omitting bad ones? Without idealizing anything, though, is there more to harvest?

Direct lessons have been drawn about development practice in research, policy influence, action learning and workshops. These are in the concluding sections of chapters.

The critical explorations in the first three chapters refer largely to personal experiences. Those in the second three are still personal but refer more to collective experiences. Let me reflect on these in turn.

Three themes

Three themes run through the first half of the book in Chapters 1, 2 and 3.

First, self-critical epistemological awareness is an ideal to struggle for. It is more easily named than known. In my early career I was not much conscious of the need for this awareness. Had I been more aware, the balance of good and bad that came from my actions would have been better. It has been a long journey and one which continues. Optimizing reflexivity and managing ego are ideals to aspire to.

Second, power plays a strong part in forming and framing knowledge. It is an elephant in the room. Self-awareness crucially has to include awareness of one's own positionality and power, of how others relate to them and to oneself, and how this affects what is presented, perceived and believed. Again, in my earlier career I was little aware of this. It was later (Chapter 3)

http://dx.doi.org/10.3362/9781780448220.007

that this was brought home by the deference I found myself receiving when perceived as powerful as a funder with the Ford Foundation. It is a pervasive and permanent problem.

Third, conviction, commitment and courage are key qualities for making a difference. Chapter 3 ends with my regret that I did not speak up more and rock the boat. I call for whistle-blowers who have access, see bad things and expose malpractice. Thirty years later it is easy to say this. At the time it was hard to do; it is the same now. We are all different. One weakness I have is wanting to be friends with everyone. I shrink from unpleasantness. For that reason among others I am no good as a manager. I leave the tough decisions and actions to others and am grateful to them for taking them. I am not proud of this and need to improve.

These three themes or threads do not stand alone. They interweave. They interplay in tensions, contradictions and synergies. Critical awareness inhibits action: more needs to be known before anything can be done. Personal and interpersonal power induce doubt and dithering: beliefs and convictions have to be probed, dissected, deconstructed and shown to be what they are – contingent, provisional, distorted. Power exacerbates misperceptions at the same time as it imposes responsibility. It is expressed both in what we do and can do and in what we choose not to do. It cannot be wished away. Ethically it has to be recognized and used. Conviction, commitment and courage demand a suspension of doubt, an acceptance of responsibility and the likelihood of some errors, bad outcomes and blame.

So we dance with these three, fumbling and stumbling, improvising steps and movements, clumsy, muddling and messing up, yet seeking redemption by struggling to optimize trade-offs, to learn, to unlearn, to make a difference, to do better. What is done, what goes wrong, whatever errors result from action – these have to be set against the counterfactual of what would have happened (or not) if nothing had been done. Unknowable counterfactuals present endless scope for comforting rationalizations to justify actions and non-actions. They also present challenges for honest and penetrating reflection and learning. None of this needs to be negative. Even ego, exhibitionism and performance can be used (wry sceptical smile) as forces for good change. Dancing can be showing off. It also explores the possible. It is good for us. To use favourite words, dancing is fulfilling and fun.

Passionate communities

The second half of the book, Chapters 4, 5 and 6, draws on personal explorations and learning, the practices of participatory workshops, and the movements of PRA and CLTS. With all these there have been many good collective experiences. With PRA and CLTS we became communities. These have differed from the Communities of Practice set up nowadays at the end of conferences and which often run into the sand or more accurately drown in a flood of emails. Moreover, PRA and CLTS have been driven by energy and are often unplanned, inspired by recurrent meetings of the like-minded, fellow enthusiasts and innovators, people with a shared sense that they were onto something, that something was unfolding, something they were part of and could give to. They were communities of colleagues, co-workers, co-conspirators almost, sensing themselves, ourselves, to be outsiders with a common vision and passion, united by a resolve to overturn walls of convention, vested interests and conservatism.

Early PRA village immersions in South India brought together a number of us who could hardly believe what was happening – the mapping, diagramming and analysis that village people showed they could do. The PRA workshop held in Bangalore in February 1991 (Mascarenhas et al., 1991) was a key moment, a tipping point, when practitioner innovators who had been scattered over different organizations and parts of India and elsewhere came together and we realized that we were not alone but a community with a common momentum and enthusiasm, and much to share . We had this sense that PRA was opening up a new world. We could not wait to learn from one another. Or take the succession of small joint IIED and IDS workshops on PRA in the early 1990s, when we picked a topic and explored where that had come to and where it could go, often leading to an issue of RRA Notes, later PLA Notes. Or the geographically isolated international workshop at Thakani in Nepal, out of contact with the rest of the world for three days, before mobile phones and three hours' walk in from the roadhead. Or take the CLTS regional sharing workshops in Lusaka and Bamako in late 2010, each with participants from a dozen countries or more which converged and coalesced to give birth to the Lusaka Declaration and the Bamako Consensus. Such a listing of events is seasoned with nostalgia and may mean little to the reader. But what I want to express is that these meetings were marked by uncertainty surely, not knowing what would happen or transpire, yet infused with excitement and openness, without academic or institutional claims of ownership, and with a feel of family who had met before.

So what were these meetings? More than what I called communities of commitment (see pages 102–3), though commitment was certainly there. Ken Robinson's (2009: 118) phrase *a passionate community* captures more of their precious essence. Using the metaphor of tribe for the like-minded with shared passion, he writes: 'When tribes gather in the same place, the opportunities for mutual inspiration can become intense. In all domains, there have been powerful groupings of people who have driven innovation through their influence on each other and the impetus they've created as a group' (Robinson, 2009: 121).

Passion says more than just enthusiasm. Many of those who met in the sharing and cogenerating days of early PRA and now with CLTS have had common experiences, care about these, and want them to spread and be adopted by others. We have felt some of the solidarity of minorities outside the mainstream, who wish to penetrate and convert that mainstream. These are indeed passionate communities. The passion gives energy and drive to find out and do more. Margaret Mead gives hope with her famous saying, 'Never doubt that a small group of thoughtful, committed citizens can change the world; indeed it's the only thing that ever has'. But the mainstreams have massive momentum. After piecemeal changes that fall short of transformation they so easily regress to a default mode. In the eternal quest for novelty, fashions change and innovations of lasting value lose the shine of novelty and are gradually superseded or forgotten. What matters then is not to give up, but to persist with vision and solidarity, and the self-fulfilling conviction of 'Yes, we can'.

The future is faster

This fits well with our contemporary context and our future. It is also in tension with it. For many of us the world of wandering around, of experiential learning, of meetings with those passionately like-minded, is on the brink of being overwhelmed by internet, email, mobile phone calls, SMS, Facebook, Twitter, video-conferencing, Skype and whatever will come next; the physical and face-to-face social worlds are in danger of being drowned by the digital.

An American economist said, 'the only thing I am sure about the future is that it will surprise me'. No doubt the certainty of this uncertainty has been a human universal since the dawn of consciousness. There may not have been many places or times when people said that change had become slower. Each age may sense that its rates of change are faster than before. Today globalization links us so much more closely that change occurs on a global scale and penetrates and affects more and more people faster and faster. Mobile phones and internet are always cited. Much is going on too through markets, media, and the interpenetration and diversity of cultures. Intensified interconnectedness means that we affect one another more than ever. Many of us are linked as never before. The butterfly effect becomes more plausible in human affairs. Or to change the metaphor, we are all aboard the same ship, tiny planet earth, collectively as vulnerable as the *Titanic*. Such clichés and truisms are so common now that familiarity with them can lure us into ignoring their recentness, significance and implications.

The accelerations of the digital revolution are most obvious for those linked in to it. Moore's Law is that the processor chips that are the backbone of every computing device double in speed every 18 months. Another law is that the amount of data coming out of fibre-optic cables, the fastest form of connectivity, doubles roughly every nine months (Schmidt and Cohen, 2013: 5). These laws may not be set in stone, but they have been validated for long enough to suggest that they are unlikely to be disproved by hitting a brick wall in the near future. So we can expect virtual capacities to continue to grow exponentially and innovations to come ever faster.

Young people born into this dual virtual–physical world have a different experience of play and exploration to that of older generations. For many of us who are better off and older, as with many of those today who are less well off, play has been and is mainly or entirely physical – games out of doors, games like chess or draughts on boards, games like hide-and-seek and charades, all involving physical interaction and invention; and much of the life of the mind has been in books. For those younger people who are now brought up half in the virtual world, these physical forms of play and living can still be there, but much more play is digital, not with people but with algorithms, screens, computer games and virtual social networking. iPads, for those whose parents can afford them, quickly become addictive. Communication with others is continuous and demanded. There is no hiding away but incessantly a desire, almost a craving, for the reassurance of being in touch.

On the positive side, an almost unlimited world of information is accessible; and the sense of play in how children experiment and try things out, exploring digital options, is embedded for life (in contrast with older people, who feel they must always get things right, and fear getting them wrong on the computer). Digitally nurtured children are becoming adults hard-wired to be experimental searchers and explorers in the virtual world. In this albeit limited sense, Dr Zeuss's observation that 'adults are obsolete children' will itself become obsolete as today's digital children become adults. As adults they will remain the digital players and explorers they became in childhood.

To many others, especially older people, this revolution presents dilemmas and choices. We have to decide whether to ride the wave of technological innovation or be left out and behind, becalmed in the peace of a bounded backwater. The decision is not easy. Just how fast things have changed is shown by what I wrote on digital tyranny only five years ago:

> A senior official of a multilateral bank received a long and imperious email from his boss in headquarters just as he was going into a morning of back-to-back meetings. When he came out of these, he found a reminder asking why he was taking so long to reply. This dominating and demoralizing use of email appears to have gone largely unremarked. Blackberry is a Trojan horse of intrusive invasion and erosion of private time and space; someone known to have one cannot hide. Hierarchy can then be strengthened, together with an orientation upwards to authority rather than downwards to poor and marginalized people. (Chambers, 2008b: 155–6)

I resolved that I would never get one. But now I have just acquired an iPhone and am no longer cut off, though writing this in the middle of a 'writing retreat' in the north-west of Scotland. Over the past 20 years Jenny and I have been coming here for periods of isolation, reflection, reading and writing. We are in the same bungalow. I am in the same room at the same table. But so much has changed. When we first came there were no mobile phones. If I wanted to communicate with anyone, it was a quarter of an hour's walk to an isolated red telephone box on a lonely road, and a struggle with pound coins until they ran out – if the phone was working; or it was by surface mail which took 48 hours to reach the south of England, and another 48 for a reply, the better part of a week. Now I sit here and deal daily with emails, and learn to explore the extraordinary repertoire of my new iPhone toy. I cannot escape. When we came here a few days ago I posted my email out-of-office sign. But I was receiving 50 messages a day. I felt I had to keep on top of them, and ought to reply to people. Also I was curious to know what was there. So I took the notice down and my office has followed me here. I have been in touch daily with colleagues in India over an 'urgent' matter. Was it urgent? I persuaded myself it was 'important'. But has this transformation been a liberation or a tyranny? Or both? It is certainly a very different way of being, thinking, playing, living, and it has crept up like a silent tide.

So does this mean that we live and learn differently, and that we have no option?

New exclusions, inclusions and impacts

To answer this question we have to ask in turn: who are the 'we'? Whose questions apply? Who gains? Who loses? Who has access? Who does not? There are conflicting tendencies. On the negative side, a majority of humankind is newly excluded. If 2 billion have some digital connectivity, 5 billion do not. It is an article of faith that soon all will be connected, that the benefits of the revolution will spread to all. This centre-outwards view seeks to extend the first to the last. Thus:

> The data revolution will bring untold benefits to the citizens of the future. They will have unprecedented insight into how other people think, behave and adhere to norms or deviate from them, both at home and in every society in the world. The newfound ability to obtain accurate and verified information online, easily, in native languages and in endless quantity, will usher in an era of critical thinking in societies around the world that before had been culturally isolated. (Schmidt and Cohen, 2013: 34)

But there are nagging questions: which citizens? And which citizens not? And where and in which countries? Schmidt and Cohen do not deal directly with poverty or inequality. Their topic and mindsets do not encompass these. Yet despite their optimism, it is hard to see how the centre-outwards – privileged centre and marginalized periphery – structure will go away. On the contrary, as it constantly evolves it constantly leaves more people out and 'behind'. Narcissistic, obsessed and absorbed by its own access, this new digital world talks to itself about itself. As more and more are mesmerized by and addicted to digital devices, so the marginalized are less visible – seen less and left out more. Inequality of access is part of the human condition and in the nature of technological innovation and dissemination. There always is and always will be a new underprivileged, a new excluded.

To be sure, there are counter-tendencies. On the positive side, the extraordinary explosion of mobile phones has transformed the lives of many – for migrants talking to their families, for a majority of people in Kenya and others elsewhere in East Africa transferring money to relatives through M-Pesa incomparably faster and more cheaply than before, for farmers and vendors keeping up to date daily, even hourly, with market conditions and prices, for more and more sick people with access to medical advice, and so on. Then we have children in rural Ethiopian villages given solar-powered laptops without instructions who have shown they can teach themselves through playful learning.[1] In terms of putting the last first, these cases leap ahead and level gradients of power and access.

There is, too, much well-rehearsed ambivalence in both positive and negative effects: activists communicating and organizing versus States seeking to control them, as famously manifest in the Arab Spring; the revelations of WikiLeaks and the gross abuses of tax evasion and avoidance in tax havens versus sophisticated systems of concealment that corporations and the wealthy can afford; mass citizen petitions and protests through sites such as Avaaz[2] and the use of internet and advertising for capitalist propaganda.[3] In the meantime, many inequalities in our world become greater and are associated with ill-being affecting not just the poorer but whole populations (Wilkinson and Pickett, 2009). True, those of us who are connected can know more about these bad things, faster and cheaper than ever before. More and more fields are open for us to explore. There are ever larger territories in which we can wander. But time, attention span and focus are ever more limited, narrowing where we go, how deeply we look, and what we have time to find.

The imperative of experiential learning

Then there is the question: what does the digital revolution do to our consciousness and our living and being?

We have to strike a balance and continuously adjust it. The dangers are clear: for some of being sucked into, mesmerized by, addicted to digital drugs; for others of failing to fend off the tyrannical tentacles of email imperatives that invade our lives; and in both cases being drawn further from the physical and social world, not least that of the poor, weak and vulnerable, of minorities, of the marginalized and excluded. Change for them too is ever faster. For those of us who are not 'them', for whom they are 'other', the challenge is to keep in touch, up-to-date, outraged and passionate. For that we have to renew explorations. We have to fight against the centripetal magnetism of the computer screen, the capital city, the 'important' visitor or meeting. We have to turn these on their heads, reverse them, and recognize that the new world for exploration is 'out there' 'with them'. As explorers we have to make ourselves vulnerable and encounter the unknown, the uncontrollable, the unforeseeable, as essential for learning. We have to expose ourselves to new experiences in the physical and social world if we are truly to learn. In this, participatory workshops can play a part. But their agendas and content must be grounded in the realities of people living in poverty. And for this there are field visits, listening surveys, citizen feedback, PPAs (participatory poverty assessments) and the like. But the most potent are also still little practised: immersions – the experiential learning of living for a few days and nights with a family in a poor community.[4] That is exploring indeed. It is both shocking and enthralling to discover how much we did not know we did not know.

Exploring as a way of living and being

Is exploring part of good living and being?

Exploration has both literal and metaphorical senses. So does explorer. I found a core identity as an explorer (see Preface). Others are and will be different. But we have multiple identities and this identity, this way of seeing oneself and of being, may work as one of multiple identities for others too. Can it provoke reflection and seeing what we do in a new and more exciting and inspiring light, and change and expand what we do? Can seeing oneself as an explorer, point to and open up ways to be more original, to branch out, to challenge and escape from ruts of routine? To go to new places and do new things? Think new thoughts?

More and more, in our turbulent, changing world, we need new ways of learning and being. I hesitate over 'new' because little is new under the sun, and there is so much deep and lasting wisdom in the great religions and literature. But so much is changing so fast that we are driven to innovate and to discover things for ourselves, and to learn better how to learn. We need some way of combining continuous creativity, innovation and adaptation. We do not always have time to search and see whether what we do is new or a rediscovery. That is how it should be. That we are finding what works for us is enough.

Exploring entails the unknown, the uncertain. We all have a pull in the other direction, towards the safe, warm womb. Faced with chaotic uncertainties, it is natural to be tense, taut, uptight. But that does not work. Is the key then an alertness that is relaxed, coming to love uncertainty and to embrace anxiety, as stimulus and opportunity for learning? I have always been nervous about uncontrollable public situations, participatory workshops included. To a degree, they are unpredictable. You have some structure and ideas, but you have to launch out and take risks. Have any of us not known that pit-of-the-stomach butterflies feeling before facilitating a workshop or a training or a participatory process with a community or group? Or before an interview? Or even just before meeting new people? What will happen? How will it work out? Will I make a fool of myself? But trying to minimize anxiety through planning, control or set sequences can blunt response, limit adaptability, miss opportunities. The paradox is that things so often work better with less planning and less control. The challenge is to find ways of being happy hosting visceral butterflies, enjoying optimal unpreparedness, and revelling in the fun of flexibility and improvisation.

Is it like white-water canoeing?[5] Faced with rapids, you do not know what you are in for. You are committed. The white water boils up around you. It is all unpredictable, risky, unstable, exhilarating. It demands intense alertness, instant adaptation, and learning, learning, learning on the run. No one else can learn for you. There are ideas in books, but you can only really learn by doing, by messing up, and trying again. And an early (and nearly late) lesson for me was that the moment you think you are through a rapid, the moment your attention wanders, that is when you tip up.

In exploratory rock climbing, there is the adrenalin of needling uncertainty. Some fear is there, but also exhilaration. No one has climbed there before. Will it go? The quality of that first experience, of that uncertainty, and with success the sense of achievement, can never be repeated. Those who do a new route name it, record the first ascent, and write up the details for a guide book. Later climbers enjoy repeating the routes, but they never have quite the same thrill of discovery.

Ordinary life is both like this and unlike it. It is like it in the uncertainty of what a day, an event or a meeting will bring, and in the uniqueness and unrepeatability of every experience. It is unlike it in that no one else can repeat or own what is both indivisible and personal, a reality of individual consciousness. There is, too, a frame of mind and way of being that can thrill at uncertainty and with awareness of the uniqueness of sequences of experience. In development practice, cannot freshness, exhilaration, novelty, and the creativity of interactions be continuous discoveries and rediscoveries for practitioners? And if so, what should we, whoever we are, whatever our identities and lives – concerned citizens, managers, practitioners, researchers, teachers, trainers, doers, thinkers – be doing now so that others can enjoy these freedoms and fulfilments? Can we all be explorers and make space for others too to explore?

There is drudgery, domination, the tyranny of procedures and requirements, restrictions of rules, limitations of resources, many, many constraints. These will always be there but in some domains, and in much international development, they seem to have got worse. Some must be endured. Many can be quietly, covertly or openly, resisted, poked fun at, manipulated, and above all made easier and lighter for others. For if we are all explorers, we should open spaces for others, and reduce and remove barriers and boundaries for them. That is perhaps the message to those who exercise controls: relax, make space, trust others, empower them, allow them to explore, take pleasure and pride in what they are then able to do.

On the other side, where there is freedom and scope, can excitement and exhilaration be a permanent part of life? Can the thrill of exploration be generic, embedded in good practice, an assured and recurring feature? Can exploration always, everywhere, have the potential to startle, amaze, excite, inspire? As when showing that things one did not dream of can be done, by people one did not believe could do them? Are we groping for an evolving way of living? Do we have in common a search for ways of being and learning that fit us better for a fulfilling life in a world of turbulent accelerating change?

We can ask what the 21st-century project should be, and what part exploring could and should have in it. Again and again we see that action and good change have been driven and inspired by imagination, commitment, critical awareness, courage, creativity and above all vision. Participatory methods, approaches, values and behaviours affirm these qualities, and express them. There is a primacy here of practice, and of experiential learning to be in touch and up to date, which revitalizes with new energy and enthusiasm and restores hope. Faith and action together expand the boundaries of the possible. Our vision can be of innumerable small personal explorations, actions and changes and how these can build up and combine to form and transform our world. The future can be brilliant if we make it so. We can all be explorers.

Gairloch, Wester Ross, Scotland

Notes

1. <www.technologyreview.com/view/429206/emtech-preview-another-way-to-think-about-learning/> [accessed 27 August 2013].
2. <http://avaaz.org/en/> [accessed 27 August 2013].
3. Arts 2 television channel on 13 September 2013 ran advertisements between movements of Ashkenazy playing Beethoven's *Hammerklavier Sonata*. One wonders where this gross insensitivity will end.
4. For PPAs see Norton et al., 2001 and Robb, 2002. For immersions see Eyben, 2004; Irvine et al., 2004; PLA, 2007; Birch and Catani, 2007. Reality Checks (Sida 2008–), started in Bangladesh and now spreading to other countries, use annual immersions as a means of keeping in touch and up-to-date with realities. Change has been found to be quite dramatically fast and unexpected.
5. See Peter Vaill's (1996) *Learning as a Way of Being: Strategies for Survival in a World of Permanent White Water*. See also page 89.

References

Absalom, E., Chambers, R., Francis, S., Gueye, B., Guijt, I., Joseph, S., Johnson, D., Kabutha, C., Rahman Khan, M., and Leurs, R. (1995) 'Participatory methods and approaches: sharing our concerns and looking to the future', *PLA Notes* 22: 5–10.

ActionAid Nepal (1992) *Participatory Rural Appraisal Utilisation Survey Report Part 1: Rural Development Area Sindhupalchowk*, Kathmandu: Monitoring and Evaluation Unit, ActionAid Nepal.

Adan, A., Brock, K., Kabakcheiva, P., Kidanu, A., Melo, M., Turk, C. and Yusuf, H. (2002) 'Who is listening? The impact of participatory poverty research on policy', in Brock and McGee (eds) *Knowing Poverty*, pp. 99–134.

Archer, D. (2007) 'Seeds of success are seeds for potential failure: Learning from the evolution of reflect', in Brock and Pettit (eds) *Springs of Participation*, pp. 15–28.

Attwood, H. and May, J. (1998) 'Kicking down doors and lighting fires: The South African PPA', in Holland with Blackburn (eds) *Whose Voice?*, pp. 119–30.

Bamako Consensus (2010) 'The Bamako CLTS Consensus: what works and traps to avoid', Regional Sharing and Learning Workshop for francophone Africa, Bamako, 29 November–3 December <www.communityledtotal sanitation.org/sites/communityledtotalsanitation.org/files/media/ Bamako_Consensus_eng_1.pdf> [accessed 27 August 2013].

Barahona, C. and Levy, S. (2003) 'How to generate statistics and influence policy using participatory methods in research: Reflections on work in Malawi 1999–2002', IDS Working Paper 212 <www.utoronto.ca/mcis/q2/ papers/IV_Barahona_Levy.pdf> [accessed 30 July 2013].

Birch, I. and Catani, R. (2007) 'Immersions: Reflections on practice', *Participatory Learning and Action* 57:134–9.

Blackburn, J. with Holland, J. (eds) (1998) *Who Changes? Institutionalizing Participation in Development*, Rugby: Practical Action Publishing.

Bongartz, P. and Chambers, R. with Kar, K. (2009) 'Beyond subsidies – triggering a revolution in rural sanitation', *IDS in Focus Policy Briefing*, Issue 10, IDS, Sussex.

Bongartz, P., Milligan, A. and Musyoki, S. (eds) (2010) 'Tales of Shit: Community-led total sanitation in Africa', *Participatory Learning and Action* 61: 27–50.

Bowen, E.S. (1956) *Return to Laughter*, London: Victor Gollanz.

Brock, K. (1999) 'It's not only wealth that matters, it's peace of mind too: A review of participatory work on poverty and illbeing', unpublished paper for *Voices of the Poor* workshop, World Bank, Washington D.C.

Brock, K. and McGee, R. (eds) (2002) *Knowing Poverty: Critical Reflections on Participatory Research and Policy*, London and Sterling, VA: Earthscan.

Brock, K. and Pettit, J. (eds) (2007) *Springs of Participation: Creating and Evolving Methods For Participatory Development*, Rugby: Practical Action Publishing <http://dx.doi.org/10.3362/9781780446004>.

Burns, D. (ed.) (2012) 'Action research for development and social change', *IDS Bulletin* 43 (3).

Buzan, T. (1974) *Use Your Head* (1989 edn), London: BBC Books.

Cernea, M. (ed.) (1985) *Putting People First: Sociological Variables in Rural Development*, Oxford: Oxford University Press for the World Bank.

Chadha, O.P. (1980) 'Consultancy services in water resources development', *Irrigation and Power Journal* (87) 4: 387–9.

Chadha, O.P. (1981) 'Irrigation system management and research priorities', *Field Research Methodologies for Improved Irrigation System Management*, Tamil Nadu Agricultural University, pp. 65–75.

Chambers, R. (1964) 'The use of case studies in public administration training in Kenya', *Journal of Local Administration Overseas* 3 (3): 169–74.

Chambers, R. (1983) *Rural Development: Putting the Last First*, Harlow: Longman.

Chambers, R. (1986) 'Canal irrigation at night', *Irrigation and Drainage Systems* 1 (1): 45–74.

Chambers, R. (1988) *Managing Canal Irrigation: Practical Analysis from South Asia*, Cambridge, UK: Cambridge University Press.

Chambers, R. (1992) 'The self-deceiving state', in R. Murray (ed.) 'New forms of public administration', *IDS Bulletin* 43 (4): 31–42.

Chambers, R. (1994) 'The origins and practice of Participatory Rural Appraisal', *World Development* 22 (7): 953–69.

Chambers, R. (1997) *Whose Reality Counts? Putting the First Last*, Rugby: Practical Action Publishing.

Chambers, R. (2002) *Participatory Workshops: A Sourcebook of 21 Sets of Ideas and Activities*, London and Stirling VA: Earthscan Publications.

Chambers, R. (2006) 'Poverty unperceived: traps, biases and agenda', *IDS Working Paper* 270, IDS, Sussex.

Chambers, R. (2008a) 'PRA, PLA and pluralism: practice and theory', in Reason and Bradbury (eds) *The Sage Handbook of Action Research*, pp. 297–318.

Chambers, R. (2008b) *Revolutions in Development Inquiry*, London and Sterling VA: Earthscan.

Chambers, R. (2010) 'Paradigms, poverty and adaptive pluralism', *IDS Working Paper* 334, IDS, Sussex <www.ibcperu.org/doc/isis/12789.pdf> [accessed 30 July 2013].

Chambers, R. (2013) 'Viewpoint – Ignorance, error and myth in South Asian irrigation: Critical reflections on experience', *Water Alternatives* 6 (2): 154–67.

Chambers, R. and Moris, J. (eds) (1973) *Mwea: An Irrigated Rice Settlement in Kenya*, Munich: Weltforum Verlag.

Chen, M., Jhabvala, R., Kanbur, R., Mirani, N. and Osner, K. (eds) (2004) *Reality and Analysis: Personal and Technical Reflections on the Working Lives of Six Women*, Working Paper for the Cornell-SEWA-WIEGO Exposure and Dialogue Program, Gujarat, 10–15 January, Department of Applied Economic and Management, Cornell University, Ithaca, New York <www.arts.cornell.edu/poverty/kanbur/EDPCompendium.pdf> [accessed 30 July 2013].

Chenevix Trench, C. (1964) *The Desert's Dusty Face*, Edinburgh and London: William Blackwood & Sons.

Clay, E. and Shaw, J. (eds) (1987) *Poverty, Development and Food: Essays in Honour of H.W. Singer on his 75th birthday*, Basingstoke and London: Macmillan Press.

Conway, G. (1985) 'Agroecosystem analysis for research and development', *Agricultural Administration* 20: 31–55.

Cornwall, A. and Pratt, G. (eds) (2003) *Pathways to Participation: Reflections on PRA*, Rugby: Practical Action Publishing <http://dx.doi.org/10.3362/9781780441276>.

Cromwell, E., Kambewa, P., Mwanza, R. and Chirwa, R. with KWERA Development Centre (2001) 'Impact Assessment Using Participatory Approaches: "Starter Pack" and Sustainable Agriculture in Malawi', *Network Paper No 112*, Agricultural Research and Extension Network, ODI London.

de Bono, E. (1981) *Atlas of Management Thinking*, Harmondsworth: Maurice Temple Smith.

Denning, S. (2000) *The Springboard: How Storytelling Ignites Action in Knowledge-Era Organizations*, Oxfordshire and New York: Butterworth and Heinemann.

Eldridge, C. (1998) 'Summary of the main findings of a PRA study on the 1992 drought in Zimbabwe', unpublished report, London: Save the Children.

Ethiopian Red Cross Society (1988) *Rapid Rural Appraisal: A Closer Look at Rural Life in Wollo*, Ethiopian Red Cross Society, London and Addis Ababa: IIED.

Evans-Pritchard, E.E. (1940) *The Nuer: A Description of the Modes of Livelihood and Political Institutions of a Nilotic People*, New York and Oxford: Oxford University Press.

Eyben, R. (2004) 'Immersions for policy and personal change', *IDS Policy Briefing* Issue 22, IDS, Sussex.

Eyben, R., Harris, C. and Pettit, J. (eds) (2006) 'Exploring power for change', *IDS Bulletin* (37) 6, November.

Fakih, M., Rahardjo, T. and Pimbert, M. with Sutoko, A., Wulandari, D. and Prasetyo, T. (2003) 'Community integrated pest management in Indonesia: Institutionalising participation and people-centred approaches', in *Institutionalising Participation and People Centred Approaches*, London: IIED, Sussex: IDS; Java, Indonesia: Research, Education and Dialogue.

Farmer, B.H. (ed.) (1977) *Green Revolution? Technology and Change in Rice-Growing Areas of Tamil Nadu and Sri Lanka*, London and Basingstoke: Macmillan.

Fuller, C. (2002) 'Training the new administration', in Johnson (ed.), *Colony to Nation*, pp. 239–43.

Gaventa, J. and Attwood, H. (1998) 'Synthesising PRA and case study materials: A participatory process for developing outlines, concepts and synthesis reports', in Participation Group *Participatory Poverty Assessments Topic Pack*, Sussex: IDS.

Gaventa, J., Creed, V. and Morrissey, J (1998) 'Scaling up: Participatory monitoring and evaluation of a federal empowerment program', *New Directions for Evaluation*, Special Issue: Understanding and Practicing Participatory Evaluation 80: 81–94 <http://dx.doi.org/10.1002/ev.1119>.

Gibson, T. (1996) *The Power in Our Hands: Neighbourhood Based – World Shaking*, Charlbury, UK: Jon Carpenter.

Gill, G.J. (1991) 'But how does it compare with the real data?' *RRA Notes 14*, pp. 5–14, London: IIED.

Groves, L. and Hinton, R. (eds) (2004), *Inclusive Aid: Changing Power and Relationships in International Development*, London: Earthscan.

Guijt, I. and Shah, M. (1998) *The Myth of Community: Gender Issues in Participatory Development*, Rugby: Practical Action Publishing.

Hanger, J. and Moris, J. (1973) 'Women and the household economy', in Chambers, R. and Moris, J. (eds), *Mwea: An Irrigated Rice Settlement in Kenya*, pp. 209–44, Munich: Weltforum Verlag.

Harrell-Bond, B.E. (1986) *Imposing Aid: Emergency Assistance to Refugees*, Oxford, New York, Nairobi: Oxford University Press.

Holdgate, M. (1958) *Mountains in the Sea: The Story of the Gough Island Expedition*, London and New York: Macmillan.

Holland, J. (ed.) (2013) *Who Counts? The Power of Participatory Statistics*, Rugby: Practical Action Publishing <http://dx.doi.org/10.3362/9781780447711>.

Holland, J. with Blackburn, J. (1998) *Whose Voice? Participatory Research and Policy Change*, Rugby: Practical Action Publishing.

Irvine, R., Chambers, R. and Eyben, R. (2004) 'Learning from poor people's experience: Immersions', *Lessons from Change in Policy & Organisations* 13, Sussex: IDS.

Johnson, J. (ed.) (2002) *Colony to Nation: British Administrators in Kenya 1940–1963*, Norfolk: The Erskine Press.

Johnson, V., Ivan-Smith, E., Gordon, G., Pridmore, P. and Patta Scott, P. (eds) (1998) *Stepping Forward: Children and Young People's Participation in the Development Process*, Rugby: Practical Action Publishing.

Jupp, D. (2004) *Views of the Poor: Some Thoughts on How to Involve Your Own Staff to Conduct Quick, Low Cost but Insightful Research into Poor People's Perspectives*, available on request from Dee Jupp email: <dee.jupp@btinternet.com>.

Kaner, S., Lind, L., Toldi, C., Fisk, S. and Berger, D. (1996) *Facilitator's Guide to Participatory Decision-Making*, Gabriola Island, BC, Canada: New Society Publishers.

Kar, K. (2003) *Subsidy or Self-Respect? Participatory Total Community Sanitation in Bangladesh*, Working Paper 184, Sussex: IDS <www.ids.ac.uk/files/Wp184. pdf> [accessed 30 July 2013].

Kar, K. (2010) *Facilitating 'Hands-on' Training Workshops for Community-Led Total Sanitation: A Trainers' Training Guide*, Geneva: Water Supply Collaborative Council <www.communityledtotalsanitation.org/sites/ communityledtotalsanitation.org/files/CLTS_trainers_training_ guide_2010.pdf> [accessed 30 July 2013].

Kar, K. and Bongartz, P. (2006) *Update on Some Recent Developments in Community-Led Total Sanitation*, Sussex: IDS <www.ids.ac.uk/files/CLTS_ update06.pdf> [accessed 1 August 2013].

Kar, K. and Pasteur, K. (2005) *Subsidy or Self-Respect? Community-Led Total Sanitation: An Update on Recent Events*, Working Paper 257, Sussex: IDS <www.communityledtotalsanitation.org/sites/communityledtotal sanitation.org/files/media/wp257_0.pdf> [accessed 30 July 2013].

Kar, K. with Chambers, R. (2008) *Handbook on Community-Led Total Sanitation*, London: Plan UK, and Sussex: IDS <www.communityledtotalsanitation. org/sites/communityledtotalsanitation.org/files/media/cltshandbook. pdf> [accessed on 30 July 2013].

Khaila, S.W., Mvula, P.M. and Kadzandira, J.M. (1999) 'Malawi: consultations with the poor', prepared for the Global Synthesis Workshop, 22–23 September, Poverty Group, PREM, World Bank, Washington DC.

KKU (1987) *Proceedings of the 1985 International Conference on Rapid Rural Appraisal*, Rural Systems Research and Farming Systems Research Projects, University of Khon Kaen, Thailand.

Kothari, Uma (ed.) (2005) *A Radical History of Development Studies: Individuals, Institutions and Ideologies*, Cape Town: David Philip; and London and New York: Zed Books.

Kotter, J.P. and Cohen, D.S. (2002) *The Heart of Change: Real-Life Stories of How People Change their Organizations*, Boston, MA: Harvard Business Review Press.

Kumar, S. (ed.) (1996) *ABC of PRA, South–South Workshop on PRA: Attitudes and Behaviour*, Bangalore and Madurai, New Delhi: PRAXIS.

Kumar, S. (ed.) (1997a) *PRA – Going to Scale: Challenges for Training, South Asia Workshop*, New Delhi: PRAXIS.

Kumar, S. (ed.) (1997b) *PRA Reflections from the Field and Practitioners*, New Delhi: PRAXIS.

Lazaro, R.C. and Wickham, T.H. (1976) 'Improvement of canal irrigation systems' facilities: Technical and management concepts', in *Proceedings of a Workshop on Implementing Public Irrigation Programmes*, Honolulu: East-West Center.

Lenton, R.L. (1983) 'Management tools for improving irrigation performance', *Discussion Paper No 5, Discussion Paper Series*, June, New Delhi: Ford Foundation.

Lilongwe Briefings (2012) Sussex: Institute of Development Studies (IDS) <www.communityledtotalsanitation.org/resource/lilongwe-briefings-outputs-international-workshop-lilongwe> [accessed 28 July 2013].

Lukenya Notes (2011) *Lukenya Notes: Taking Community Led Total Sanitation to Scale with Quality – Outputs from a workshop in Nairobi, Kenya, 24th–27th July 2011*, Sussex: IDS <www.communityledtotalsanitation.org/resource/lukenya-notes-taking-clts-scale-quality> [accessed 28 July 2013].

Lusaka Declaration (2010) Regional Sharing and Learning Workshop of CLTS: Lusaka <www.communityledtotalsanitation.org/sites/communityledtotal sanitation.org/files/Lusaka_declaration.pdf> [accessed 28 July 2013].

Lytle, P. (1999) *Consultations with the Poor, Site Report, Bosnia-Sarajevo*, World Bank, Washington DC.

Malhotra, S.P. (1982) *The Warabandi System and its Infrastructure*, India Central Board of Irrigation and Power, Publication no. 157, New Delhi.

Mascarenhas, J., Shah, P., Joseph, S., Jayakaran, R., Devavaram, J., Ramachandran, V., Fernandez, A., Chambers, R., Pretty, J. (1991) *Proceedings of the February 1991 Bangalore PRA Trainers Workshop*, RRA Notes 13, London: IIED; Bangalore: MYRADA.

McGee, R. (2002) 'The self in participatory poverty research', in Brock and McGee (eds), *Knowing Poverty*, pp. 14–43, London: Earthscan.

McGee, R. and Brock, K. (2001) 'From Poverty Assessment to Policy Change: Processes, Actors and Data', *IDS Working Paper* 133, Sussex: IDS.

Mehta, L. and Movik, S. (eds) (2011) *Shit Matters: The Potential of Community-Led Total Sanitation*, Rugby: Practical Action Publishing <http://dx.doi.org/10.3362/9781780440347>.

Melo, M. (1999) *Consultation with the Poor: Brazil – National Synthesis Report*, The World Bank, Washington DC.

Morse, B. and Berger, T.R. (1992) *Sardar Sarovar: Report of the Independent Review*, pp. 349–58, Ottawa: Resource Futures International Inc; Switzerland: International Environmental Law Research Centre.

Moser, C. (2001) "Apt illustration' or 'anecdotal information'? Can qualitative data be representative or robust?', prepared for the Qualitative-Quantitative Poverty Appraisal Workshop, 15–16 March, Cornell University, Ithaca, New York.

Mukherjee, N. (1995) *Participatory Rural Appraisal and Questionnaire Survey: Comparative Field Experience and Methodological Innovations*, New Delhi: Concept Publishing.

Nainital Statement (2013) National Workshop on Community-Led Approaches to Sanitation in the context of Nirmal Bharat Abhiyan <www.communityledtotalsanitation.org/sites/communityledtotalsanitation.org/files/Nainital_statement.pdf> [accessed 30 July 2013].

Nandago, M. (2007) 'Training and facilitation: the propellers of participatory methodologies', in Brock and Pettit (eds), *Springs of Participation: Creating and Evolving Methods For Participatory Development*, pp. 29–39, Rugby: Practical Action Publishing <http://dx.doi.org/10.3362/9781780446004.003>.

Narayan, D. and Petesch, P. (eds) (2002) *Voices of the Poor: From Many Lands*, Oxford: Oxford University Press; New York: The World Bank.

Narayan, D., Chambers, R., Shah, M.K. and Petesch, P (1999) 'Global Synthesis: Consultations with the Poor', prepared for the Global Synthesis Workshop, 22–23 September, Poverty Group, PREM, World Bank, Washington DC.

Narayan, D., with Patel, R., Schafft, K., Rademacher, A. and Koch-Schulte, S. (2000a) *Voices of the Poor: Can Anyone Hear Us?* Oxford University Press for New York: The World Bank.

Narayan, D., Chambers, R., Shah, M.K. and Petesch, P. (2000b) *Voices of the Poor: Crying out for Change*, Oxford University Press for New York: The World Bank.

Norton, A., with Bird, B., Brock, K., Kakande, M. and Turk, C. (2001) *A Rough Guide to PPAs: Participatory Poverty Assessment: An Introduction to Theory and Practice*, London: Overseas Development Institute.

Osner, K. (2004) 'Using exposure methodology for dialogue on key issues', in Chen et al. (eds), *Reality and Analysis: Personal and Technical Reflections on the Working Lives of Six Women*, Working Paper for the Cornell-SEWA-WIEGO Exposure and Dialogue Program, Gujarat, 10–15 January.

Owen, H. (2008) *Open Space: A User's Guide*, 3rd edn, San Francisco: Berret-Koehler.

PLA (2004) *Critical Reflections, Future Directions*, Participatory Learning and Action 50, October <http://pubs.iied.org/9440IIED.html?t=PLA+50> [accessed 28 August 2013].

PLA (2007) *Immersions: Learning About Poverty Face-to-Face*, Participatory Learning and Action 57, December <http://pubs.iied.org/search.php?k=pla+57> [accessed 28 August 2013].

Pontius, J., Dilts, R. and Bartlett, A. (eds) (2002) *From Farmer Field School to Community IPM; Ten Years of IPM Training in Asia*, Bangkok: FAO Regional Office for Asia and the Pacific.

Praxis (1999) *Consultations with the Poor: India 1999, Country Synthesis Report*, Consultations with the Poor, prepared for Global Synthesis Workshop, 22–23 September 1999, Poverty Group, PREM, Washington DC: World Bank.

Rademacher, A. and Patel, R. (2002) 'Retelling worlds of poverty: Reflections on transforming participatory research for a global narrative', in Brock and McGee (eds), *Knowing Poverty*, pp. 166–88, London and Sterling VA: Earthscan.

Rahmatu, D. and Kidanu, A. (1999) *Ethiopia, Consultations with the Poor: A Study to Inform the World Development Report 2000/01 on Poverty and Development*, Washington DC: World Bank.

Reason, P. and Bradbury, H. (eds) (2008) *The Sage Handbook of Action Research*, 2nd edn, Los Angeles, London, New Delhi, Singapore: Sage Publications.

Reflect (1994) *Education Action* <www.reflect-action.org/educationaction> [accessed 27 August 2013].

Repetto, R. (1986) *Skimming the Water: Rent-seeking and the Performance of Public Irrigation Systems*, Washington: World Resources Institute, December.

Rhoades, R. (1982) *The Art of the Informal Agricultural Survey*, Lima: International Potato Center.

Richards, P. (1985) *Indigenous Agricultural Revolution*, London: Hutchinson and Colorado: Westview Press.

Robb, C. (2002) *Can the Poor Influence Policy? Participatory Poverty Assessments in the Developing World*, 2nd edn, Washington DC: International Monetary Fund and The World Bank.

Robinson, K., with Aronica, L. (2009) *The Element: How Finding Your Passion Changes Everything*, London: Penguin Books.

Schmidt, E. and Cohen, J. (2013) *The New Digital Age: Reshaping the Future of People, Nations and Business*, London: John Murray.

Schulz, K. (2010) *Being Wrong: Adventures in the Margin of Error*, London: Portobello Books.

Seckler, D. and Joshi, D. (1982) 'Sukhomajri: Water Management in India', *Bulletin of Atomic Scientists* 38: 26–30.

Shah, T. (1993) *Groundwater Markets and Irrigation Development: Political Economy and Practical Policy*, Bombay, Delhi, Calcutta, Madras: Oxford University Press.

Sida (2008, 2009, 2010, 2011, 2012) *Reality Check Bangladesh 2007, 2008, 2009, 2010, 2011* (respectively), Stockholm: Sida and GRM International. The last three reports are available at <http://reality-check-approach.com/reality-checks/bangladesh> [accessed 28 August 2013].

SDC (2003) *Views of the Poor: The Perspectives of Rural and Urban Poor in Tanzania As Recounted Through their Stories and Pictures*, Berne: SDC.

Taylor, P. and Fransman, J. (2003) *Learning to Participate: The Role of Higher Learning Institutions as Development Agents*, IDS Policy Briefing, Issue 20, Sussex: IDS.

unNabi, R., Dipankara, D., Chakrabarty, S., Begum, M. and Chaudhury, N.J. (1999) *Consultation with the Poor: Participatory Poverty Assessment in Bangladesh*, prepared for Global Synthesis Workshop, 22–23 September, Washington DC: World Bank.

Vaill, P.B. (1996) *Learning as a Way of Being: Strategies for Survival in a World of Permanent White Water*, San Francisco: Jossey-Bass.

VeneKlasen, L. with Miller, V. (2002) *A New Weave of Power, People and Politics: The Action Guide for Advocacy and Citizen Participation*, Oklahoma City: World Neighbours.

Waddington, C.H. (1977) *Tools for Thought*, St Albans: Paladin.

Wade, R. (1982) 'The system of administrative and political corruption: Canal irrigation in South India', *Journal of Development Studies* 18: 287–328.

Wade, R. and Chambers, R. (1980) 'Managing the main system: Canal irrigation's blind spot', *Economic and Political Weekly* 15: A107–12.

Watts, J., Mackay, R., Horton, D., Hall, A., Douthwaite, B., Chambers, R. and Acosta, A. (2003) *Institutional Learning and Change: An Introduction*,

Discussion Paper 03-10, October, The Hague: International Service for National Agricultural Research.

Wickham, T. and Valera, A. (1978) 'Practices and accountability for better water management', in *Irrigation Policy and Management in Southeast Asia*, pp. 61–75, Philippines: IRRI.

Wickham, T., Giron, D., Valera, A. and Mejia, A. (1974) 'A field comparison of rotational and continuous irrigation in the Upper Pampanga River Project', paper presented at Saturday seminar, 3 August 1994, Philippines: International Rice Research Institute.

Wilkinson, R. and Pickett, K. (2009) *The Spirit Level: Why More Equal Societies Almost Always Do Better*, London: Allen Lane, Penguin Press.

Wolfensohn, J. (1999) 'Coalitions for change', address to the Board of Governors of the World Bank, 28 September.

World Bank (1999) *Consultations with the Poor: Process Guide for the 20 Country Study for the World Development Report 2000/01*, Poverty Group, PREM Network, Washington DC: The World Bank.

World Bank (2000) *Poverty and Development: The World Development Report 2000/01: Attacking Poverty*, New York and Oxford: Oxford University Press.

Yates, J. and Okello, L. (2002) 'Learning from Uganda's efforts to learn from the poor: Reflections and lessons from the Uganda Participatory Poverty Assessment Project', in Brock and McGee (eds), *Knowing Poverty: Critical Reflections on Participatory Research and Policy*, pp. 14–43, London and Sterling, VA: Earthscan.

Index